HOW TO READ A ROOM

Other Books by Mike Bechtle

The Introvert's Guide to Success in the Workplace

One-Minute Tips for Confident Communication

It's Better to Bite Your Tongue Than Eat Your Words

The People Pleaser's Guide to Loving Others without Losing Yourself

Dealing with the Elephant in the Room

I Wish He Had Come with Instructions

People Can't Drive You Crazy If You Don't Give Them the Keys

How to Communicate with Confidence

Evangelism for the Rest of Us

HOW TO READ A ROOM

Navigate Any Situation, Lead with Confidence, and Create an Impact at Work

DR. MIKE BECHTLE

a division of Baker Publishing Group
Grand Rapids, Michigan

Published by Revell
a division of Baker Publishing Group
Grand Rapids, Michigan
RevellBooks.com

Printed in the United States of America

Library of Congress Cataloging-in-Publication Data
Names: Bechtle, Mike, 1952– author.
Title: How to read a room : navigate any situation, lead with confidence, and create an impact at work / Dr. Mike Bechtle.
Description: Grand Rapids, Michigan : Revell, [2025] | Includes bibliographical references.
Identifiers: LCCN 2024018734 | ISBN 9780800742782 (paperback) | ISBN 9780800746773 (casebound) | ISBN 9781493448678 (ebook)
Subjects: LCSH: Interpersonal communication. | Confidence. | Awareness. | Success in business.
Classification: LCC BF637.C45 B42947 2025 | DDC 650.1—dc23/eng/20240703
LC record available at https://lccn.loc.gov/2024018734

The names and details of the people and situations described in this book have been changed or presented in composite form in order to ensure the privacy of those with whom the author has worked.

Cover design by Ervin Serrano

Baker Publishing Group publications use paper produced from sustainable forestry practices and postconsumer waste whenever possible.

25 26 27 28 29 30 31 7 6 5 4 3 2

To Kezia

You enter every room,
then you brighten it.
Nobody lights up the room
like *you*!

CONTENTS

Introduction 9

1. Why It Matters 13

Part 1 The Three Essentials (for Success) 21

2. Master Your Mindset—*You Can Do This* 25
3. Master the Process—*It's Worth the Effort* 35
4. Master Your Perceptions—*You Can Learn to See Others Accurately* 45

Part 2 How to Read a Room (for Confidence) 57

5. Observe the Setting, Part 1—*Get the Big Picture* 61
6. Observe the Setting, Part 2—*Get the Small Picture* 69
7. Engage with People, Part 1—*Connect with Anyone* 81
8. Engage with People, Part 2—*Converse with Anyone* 91
9. Plan Your Approach—*Customize Your Strategy* 103
10. Execute Your Strategy—*Work the Room* 115

Part 3 How to Lead a Room (for Influence) 125

11. Leading the Room 129
12. Leading by Influence in a Virtual Room 139
13. Leading by Influence from the Front of the Room 151
14. Leading by Influence through Written Communication 163

Part 4 How to Serve a Room (for Impact) 173

15. The Life-Changing Vision for Serving a Room 177
16. The Challenge of Change 185
17. Ten Steps Down into Greatness 193
18. Legacy Time 205

Conclusion 211
Acknowledgments 213
Notes 217

INTRODUCTION

I'm surprised I didn't get fired.

After grad school I landed my first "real" job: teaching at a small college in Arizona. I knew the subject well, but I didn't have much experience in the classroom. I just figured I could stand up front and tell them what I knew. My job was to teach, and their job was to learn. If they didn't learn, their grades would reflect their lack of effort. It was their problem, not mine.

Whenever I entered the classroom, I tried to "read the room." I always saw two groups of students. One group was already excited about the topic and couldn't wait to learn. They made my job fun because they brought their excitement and energy into the classroom every day. They probably would have learned the subject whether I showed up or not.

Then I would see the other group: those who were indifferent about the subject but needed to pass in order to graduate. They made my job challenging because each class session seemed like an unavoidable delay in their day. They were committed to doing the minimum possible amount of work to pass, assuming they would never use the subject in the real world.

In my first few years of teaching, I focused on the first group. I figured that my energy should go to those who made the effort. I mostly ignored the others, believing they didn't care and wouldn't do well in the class.

Then I had a paradigm shift and learned to read the room differently.

It came during an informal discussion I had with some friends over dinner one night. We started talking about the best and worst teachers we'd experienced in school. Everyone agreed that the worst teachers were the ones who didn't care if we learned what they were teaching or not. They were just experts who expected us to listen, take notes, and memorize the details of the topic. Their whole focus was on the content, not on us.

The best teachers were those who were so passionate about the subject that they leaked enthusiasm. They knew that if we could catch the vision of what that knowledge would do for us, it would become contagious, and we'd be motivated to learn on our own. They cared deeply about all their students, and they believed their role was to be a catalyst, not a dictator. They would light the fuse, and we would catch on fire.

Previously, I'd followed the normal way of entering and reading a room: look around, make assumptions about what's going on, believe those assumptions, and fend for myself. I wasn't trying to make a difference in the room; I was concerned primarily with myself. I needed to survive and feel OK in that environment.

During that meal, I came to realize I wasn't just in that classroom for myself. I was there for other people—all of them. I needed different lenses to read that room. Sure, I wanted to feel comfortable, but I also wanted to feel confident that I could make a difference. That's why I was there—not just so the students would see me as a good teacher but would become better people because we got to spend time together.

From that point on, I became passionate about reading the room so I could impact my students' lives. It was my chance to move from the "worst teacher" list to the "best teacher" list by looking outward instead of just inward.

Once I learned how easy it would be to adopt this new paradigm, my whole career turned the corner. From that moment on, I shifted from insecurity to impact.

And so can you.

CHAPTER 1

Why It Matters

Most people don't wake up in the middle of the night wishing they knew how to read a room. They worry about having enough money to pay for that unexpected car repair, or about the details of a project they're in charge of, or the poor choices a family member is making. Such thoughts are always about fear or pain or what could go wrong, not about what could go right. To make it worse, everything seems exaggerated in the middle of the night, right? Fears are more frightening, pain is more painful, and family situations seem hopeless.

Learning to read a room isn't usually a big concern for us unless we just came out of a situation that didn't go well. Some of us can be uncomfortable because, as introverts, navigating events doesn't come naturally. Others of us are OK with making small talk, but it feels like we're wasting our time. If we're a leader, we want to communicate well but can't always tell if anybody is paying attention.

For most of us, reading a room usually falls in the category of "a nice skill to have" versus "I need to drop everything and learn that skill now." The only way we'll commit to learning these skills is to have a clear focus on the payoff—how things could be different.

Here are two simple questions that will give us the answer we're looking for:

1. What will happen if I learn how to read a room well?
2. What will happen if I don't?

Let's explore those questions, then look at what keeps us from going after these skills.

Reading a Room—the Upsides and Downsides

Learning to read a room well isn't a skill that's reserved for certain outgoing, gregarious people. It's something anyone can learn, regardless of their temperament. When you master the simple skills, here's what you'll be able to do:

- You'll walk into every new situation with confidence, seeing each encounter as an adventure to be explored.
- You'll know the exact framework for figuring out what's going on and what to do in every situation.
- You won't have to "work the room" like a high-pressure salesperson; you'll get to be 100 percent yourself.
- You'll be able to discover exactly what people need and respond appropriately, so your influence will increase.
- People will come to respect you—not because of how you've come across but how you've made them better.

What are the downsides of *not* knowing how to read a room? Here are a few of the risks:

- Misunderstandings: feeling uncertain about what people are thinking and making the wrong assumptions.
- Missed opportunities: losing the chance to connect with people who could benefit you in the future.
- Awkwardness: being worried about what people think of you, which gets in the way of you thinking about them.
- Professional limitations: interfering with your chances for advancement by being unable to read a room.
- Unproductive leadership: finding yourself in charge of mediocre meetings, underwhelming presentations, and informal conversations that feel shallow.

How does this work? In general, all of us fit into two broad categories:

1. Those who are comfortable walking into a room.
2. Those who are uncomfortable walking into a room.

If you're in the first group, you might not even be reading this book. You enjoy group settings, so you don't have a strong sense of need. You're probably more on the extroverted side, so you look forward to having more people to interact with. You're energized by being intentional around others, and that energy increases the longer you're there.

That's OK, because there's nothing wrong with enjoying yourself. At the same time, there's a difference between feeling *comfortable* and feeling *confident*. Feeling comfortable benefits *you*, because you're not feeling intimidated. That doesn't mean, however, that you're making the most of the situation. When you're confident, it benefits *others*. It means you've developed the skills to recognize what's happening in the room and how you can make it better.

The fact that you picked up this book probably puts you in the second group. Most likely, you're a bit more introverted, and you're concerned about how you're coming across and what others are thinking of you. Your biggest felt need is to feel more comfortable.

That's a legitimate concern. The easiest way to become comfortable in a room is to become competent with the process—knowing how to read the room, recognize what's happening in the room, and have accurate data to work with. When you have the skills to read a room, you'll feel confident entering the room.

A Skillset You Can Master

We all walk into situations where we don't know what to expect:

- We go to the conference room to present a change in our team's compensation plan, wondering how they'll respond.
- We're in a virtual meeting, waiting for the HR manager to make a major announcement about the company's remote work policy, and we wonder how it will impact us.
- We show up at a company barbecue where we can't avoid the people who always know how to push our buttons.
- Our boss summons us to their office, and we don't know why.

We all know how it feels to enter a situation, take in information, and wonder what to do next. We wish we knew instinctively how to respond in the moment, but our tank of ideas is empty.

Perhaps there is a weekly meeting to attend at work. Some people hope they'll get something out of it, others are energized by that weekly session, and the rest count the minutes until it ends.

In another company, an executive shows up at one of the field offices to announce a restructuring that will affect everyone, knowing there will probably be some pushback. Meanwhile, across town, a sales representative makes a presentation to a procurement team to win their business, while a manager at that location meets with their employees to set goals for the upcoming season.

Every day, you and I face situations like these—and it's not just at work:

- At the grocery store, you study the length of each checkout line and how much each person has in their cart to decide which line to join (and you're frustrated when you picked the one where someone has a stack of coupons and is counting their coins to pay).
- You pull into the driveway after a long flight, looking forward to reconnecting and relaxing. As you open the door, it's too quiet, and you sense the tension in the air (even the dog is cowering in the corner). Something's up, and you need to figure out what it is.
- You recently joined the board of your homeowner's association, and you're attending your first meeting. You're the newbie, as the other members have been together for years. You want to show your competence while respecting their experience. It's time to observe the interpersonal dynamics so you'll know how to make an impact.

What's the common ground in all of those settings? We read each "room," trying to assess the situation and make good decisions based on what we can see.

A person entering a room tries to figure out what's going on. In a physical room, they notice who's sitting and who's standing;

who's smiling and who's frowning; who looks angry or bored and who looks energized; who is talking to who. In a virtual meeting room, they're studying those who have their cameras on, trying to guess if they're listening or if they're checking email or playing online solitaire. Based on those observations, they make assumptions about what's happening in the room and then decide what to do next.

But their assumptions could be totally wrong. And if they don't know what to look for, their chances of being wrong are even greater.

Here's the good news: *reading a room is a skill that anyone can learn* using a four-step process that works in *any* situation.

1. *Observe the setting*. Discover what's *really* happening in the room.
2. *Engage with people*. Converse with curiosity and purpose.
3. *Plan your approach*. Determine a simple framework for effectiveness.
4. *Execute your strategy*. Take action on your discoveries to impact the room.

This simple process consistently leads to a successful outcome. It moves you from indecisive confusion to confident action, giving you the ability to respond with confidence in any situation. It doesn't matter what your temperament or personality is like, whether you're the formal leader of a group or if people even know who you are. You'll know exactly how to read any room—and how to make a difference.

A New Approach

I've read dozens of books on this subject to prep for writing this one. Most tell you how to read the room so you can take charge, be the charismatic leader in the room, and get people to admire you. It seems like they're emphasizing how to get people to like you so you won't feel intimidated in those situations.

This book is different. Yes, you'll learn how to observe what's going on and interpret it accurately. That's the easy part. But you'll have a deeper motive than making yourself look and feel better; you'll look for ways to make others' lives better.

Isn't that really what we want in life? It's nice to have people think well of us, but that alone isn't satisfying in the long run. When we build skills that enable us to serve others, we embark on a lifetime of fulfillment because we're looking outward instead of inward.

Want to change the world? You can—by impacting those around you. If you enter every room with the mindset of making it better, you'll motivate others to do the same with the people around them. Like a pebble tossed into a pond, the ripple effect grows exponentially because you took the initiative.

The Journey

This book is a combination of the latest research plus my own experience leading seminars for over thirty years. I've walked into over three thousand conference rooms and auditoriums, never knowing what I'd find. From those experiences, I gradually learned what to do as I came through the door, what to look for, and how to accurately size up the needs of individuals as they arrived. Over time, the process became automatic. I knew exactly how to approach and analyze each new room (reading for confidence), how to help people learn new skills and implement them (leading for results), and how to genuinely motivate each person in the room to grow into their personal best (serving for impact).

Most of what I learned came through trial and error—mostly error. It seems like most of the wisdom we have in life comes through the mistakes we make, right? Hopefully, we learn from those mistakes and gain competence.

I remember trying to help my then-teenage daughter, Sara, learn from my mistakes to save her the pain of experiencing them on her own. She said, “But, Daddy—I want to make my own mistakes.”

I’ll tell you what I’ve learned through both my mistakes and my successes. Mostly, I’ll share principles I’ve learned over the years through a wide variety of situations, principles you’ll be able to incorporate into your own journey to make a difference. It will be a practical and experiential approach to confidence and success. Sure, you’ll make your own mistakes, but maybe you can learn a few things from mine too—and we can grow from celebrating each other’s successes.

You’ll learn a step-by-step process that’s simple and repeatable in any situation. You’ll know exactly what to look for, and you’ll know what to do next.

The result? You’ll work within your natural temperament to feel completely confident walking into any room because you’ve been trained. Whether you’re a reflective introvert or an outgoing extrovert, you get to be 100 percent yourself. You won’t worry about how you’re coming across; you’ll design your own unique process to serve the people you encounter and make their lives better.

Confidence, influence, and impact. Doesn’t that sound great? It won’t be hard at all once you know what to do. You’ll learn it easily, and it’ll quickly become second nature the more you practice. Over time, you’ll be the one in the room who knows what’s really happening and how to make it better.

Join me in this adventure. I’ll walk with you on the entire path, and we’ll do this together.

I know how this will turn out. And I promise you’ll be glad you came along on this journey!

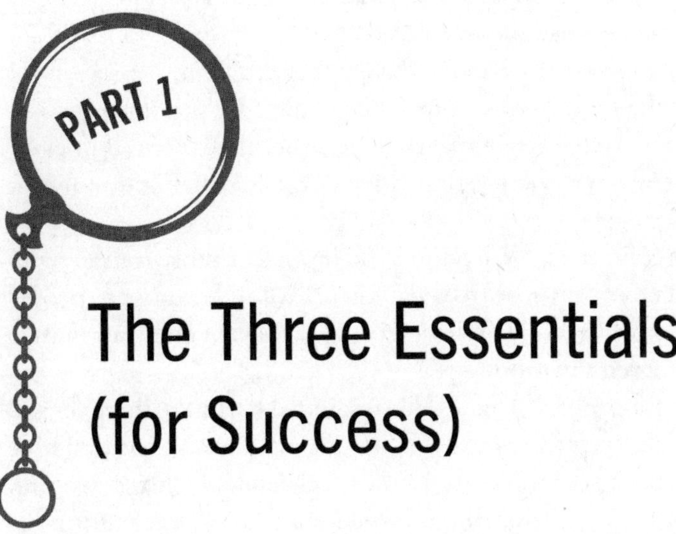

The Three Essentials (for Success)

When I wrote this section, I was sitting in the outdoor seating area of a unique, local coffee shop outside of Nashville. It's a large, grassy area outside a historic building, lush with hedges and flowers and massive old trees that provide shade. For an author, it's the perfect setting to feel inspired.

I settled in at a small, square wooden table with my coffee and set up my laptop. As I placed my fingers on the keys, leaning my forearms on the table, the table rocked slightly toward me, and a small splash of coffee made a puddle around my cup. I grabbed a couple of napkins to clean it up, then tried to keep working. But I quickly realized I was on uneven ground, and the problem would continue.

I tried a couple of other tables but found the same issue. It was a great atmosphere, but I wanted to drink my coffee, not clean tables with it. I didn't want to leave, but I needed something more stable so I could focus without distraction.

One of the employees was making the rounds of the outside tables, making sure everyone was OK. I guess she noticed my dilemma because she wandered over to offer help. Evidently, it wasn't the first time she had seen this problem. "Sorry about that," she said. "Those four-legged tables are OK for conversation, but not for getting work done. Since the ground is uneven, there's always one leg that doesn't quite reach and makes it rock."

She continued, "Why don't you try one of those round three-legged tables by those trees over there? We added those so people could work outside. With three legs, they sit solid no matter how uneven the ground is."

She was right. My new table reminded me of the three-legged stools dairy farmers use when milking cows by hand. Three legs make it solid no matter how much a person moves around.

Not only was that three-legged table a perfect solution for my writing but it also supplied a perfect introduction to this section. If we're going to learn to read a room well, we need a solid framework in our approach to learning these skills. That's what this section is about, and we'll make sure we have the right table.

This book will provide the solid framework for confidence and impact in any room you enter. But if you ignore that framework, these techniques won't become part of who you are; they'll be tacked on, and you'll be *acting* confident instead of *being* confident. Constant pretending is exhausting, so let's avoid it.

That's why we're starting with this three-legged table to get our framework firmly in place:

1. *We need to think clearly about our mindset*, believing that it's possible to gain these skills. It's all about how to become proactive, taking responsibility for personal growth and change.

2. *We need to think clearly about the process*: what it involves, what it doesn't involve, and why it's worth discovering and mastering.
3. *We need to think clearly about others*, recognizing our natural biases for each person we meet and learning to genuinely value the uniqueness of others.

Every room will be different, which is the uneven ground. This section is critical for enabling us to move confidently into any situation. Skip this framework, and all the techniques will become ineffective over time. Master this preparation, and success is guaranteed.

We don't just want to look better in the rooms we enter. We want to *be* better—having the confidence and skill to make a difference. It's an inside-out job. Let's jump into the inside work first in these next three chapters.

CHAPTER 2

Master Your Mindset

You Can Do This

The vast population of this earth . . . may readily be divided into three groups. There are the few who make things happen, the many more who watch things happen, and the overwhelming majority who have no notion of what happens.

Nicholas Murray Butler

"We need some fresh ideas for making our customers happy," the boss says. "Let's have a brainstorming session in our next meeting to see what we can come up with."

What goes through your head when you hear that? Most people find themselves in one of two categories:

1. *Brainstorming? I don't know if I'm good at that, but it'll be a great chance to learn how to do it. Sounds like a great opportunity to grow!*
2. *I'm horrible at brainstorming. I'm just not creative, and I can never think of anything to add. Other people are good at it, but not me. Maybe I can call in sick that day.*

Some of us see new opportunities as a way to grow and gain new skills. Others think that we're "just who we are," so there's no hope of changing or growing or becoming anything different. It's our mindset—how we see ourselves. Either way, there could be a lot of reasons for it, but you've probably had one or the other mindset since you were a kid. Over time, you settled into a pattern that worked for you, and it's your default setting today.

Psychologist and author Carol Dweck describes these two categories as having a *growth mindset* or a *fixed mindset*. A *growth mindset* says that our basic qualities and intelligence can be developed through personal effort, strategies, and help from others. People with this mindset believe they grow throughout life by their choices, and there's no limit to how far they can go.

A *fixed mindset* suggests that we're born with a certain amount of intelligence, and it never changes. People with this mindset feel the need to constantly prove their intelligence, so they ask themselves, "Will I succeed or fail? Will I look smart or dumb? Will I be accepted or rejected? Will I feel like a winner or a loser?"[1] Since they don't believe they can get smarter or better, they're concerned primarily about how others see them. They're into positioning more than performing.

What's this have to do with learning to read a room? *Everything.*

A Deeper Perspective

If you have a growth mindset about reading a room, you'll be able to develop your skills and find confidence in any situation. If you have a fixed mindset, you believe that you'll never really get good at it, and you'll never feel confident. You'll always be pretending to feel comfortable, and it will exhaust you.

Here's the good news: *you can change your mindset.*

When it comes to finding success in any endeavor, mindset is "Job #1." It's nonnegotiable—and it's something we can choose. Nothing matters more than our mindset. If we don't have the right mindset, all the tips and techniques for reading a room will be irrelevant. We might try them out, but it'll always feel forced because we haven't changed the way we think.

When your mindset changes, *everything changes*.

Let's expand this by looking at a second perspective that builds on the growth mindset versus fixed mindset idea. It's the concept of becoming proactive versus being reactive.

A *reactive* person sees life through a victim mentality. Everything that happens is out of their control, and it never occurs to them that they could do anything differently. They're at the mercy of other people's actions and choices, and this determines the way they feel. If anything is going to get better, the other person will have to change. After all, the other person is the problem, and they're messing everything up.

A *proactive* person takes responsibility for their attitude and actions. They determine what they can control and put their energy and focus there. For the things they can't control, they learn to accept and adapt. When faced with a challenge, their first thought is, *So, what can I do in this situation?*

If you want to learn how to read a room and impact that room, you'll need to switch from being reactive to being proactive. If you're reactive, you'll see your role as being a chameleon—changing your behavior to fit in with whatever is happening around you. You won't be yourself because you'll be crafting an image for others to see. You'll never become confident because you've given everyone else the power over your emotions.

Author Stephen R. Covey often shared how reactive people feel good if the weather is good, and they feel bad if the weather is bad. How they feel is tied to whatever is happening around them. By contrast, "Proactive people carry their own weather with them."[2] If you're proactive, you take responsibility for the way you feel and respond as well as the choices you make.

Proactivity means focusing on the things you have control over instead of the things you can't control. It also moves you away from being a victim of your circumstances to making a difference in your circumstances. It's a bias for action, and it's something you can choose to do.

Here's how it plays out at work. Say you've been assigned to a project team with several other people. In the first meeting, the key stakeholder presents their expectations for the project. Everyone takes notes and begins working on the project. Soon, questions come up about the details of what the outcome should look like, and everyone is trying to figure out what to do.

The reactive team members might argue that the stakeholder should have been clearer. They're frustrated that they have to figure it out, so they guess what should happen and hope for the best, grumbling the whole time about the sketchy details.

The proactive team members go back to the stakeholder and ask for clarification. In fact, they would have sought that clarification in the initial meeting, asking questions like:

"When you say you want the project to be successful, what does that look like to you?"

"You said it can't cost too much. Can you give us an idea of what that would look like in dollars?"

"How often would you like a progress report, to make sure we're on track with your expectations?"

Reactive people wait for events to occur and then respond to them. Proactive people anticipate problems before they occur and actively work to find solutions.

Reactive people let circumstances dictate their actions. Proactive people work on getting what they want, being intentional about their choices and responses.

The Benefits of Proactivity

My wife and I have always done our own yardwork. We mow, we trim, we dig, and we water. We'll often spend a whole Saturday bringing our landscape under control. It's a lot of work, but it feels great at the end of the day to see the results.

The final step is always cleaning up the mess we've made on the sidewalks. They're always covered with grass and clippings and leaves and whatever else is leftover from our efforts. It's not our favorite part of the job, but it's essential. For years, we would grab a couple of brooms and go to work.

A couple of years ago, we bought a small electric leaf blower with money my wife's dad gave us for our anniversary. We weren't sure we needed it because the brooms worked, but we knew others who had blowers and thought they were great. So, we tried it. It was like *magic*. It cleaned up the mess in a fraction of the time and did a much better job. Now we can't imagine doing yardwork without it.

When we only had brooms, they worked—so we really didn't see a need to do it any other way. But now that we've experienced the benefits of the leaf blower, we'll never go back. It's one of the best investments we've ever made.

Learning to be proactive might sound like a lot of work, right? Do we really need to make that change? If we can see the benefits, the answer will be a resounding "Yes!"—and it can change everything. Here's why proactivity is worth pursuing.

You stay ahead of the game

Think of a project you have that seems overwhelming. Reactivity follows the path of least resistance—procrastinating, getting distracted, waiting until the last minute, and getting frustrated. You tell people, "I work best under pressure." Proactivity happens when you start early, plan your time carefully, and take one small step at a time. You'll feel confident throughout the project, even if it's challenging, and you'll accomplish more than you thought was possible.

You gain a sense of control

When our kids were teenagers, we would take them on family vacations. For a few years, they complained the whole time because they wanted to do something different or stay in a different hotel, and they felt like victims of our choices. Finally, we decided to teach them how to be proactive and turned the planning over to them. "Here's how much money you have to work with, and here is the time frame. Here's a map. You get to decide where we go, where we'll stay, and what we'll do. We'll help you think through the details as much as you need us to, but you're in charge." We "forced" them to be proactive, and it turned out great. They couldn't complain about anything since it had all been their decision. They learned quickly about the payoff of proactivity, and we had some of the best vacations ever.

You avoid stress

A tire blows out on your car, and replacing it is going to be expensive. How do you feel if you have enough in your bank account to cover it but nothing extra? You're stressed. How do you feel if you have $50,000 in your account? You're not stressed. Proactivity helps you anticipate problems so you can either prevent them or minimize them. Becoming proactive helps you overcome procrastination, so you'll have more margin—which means you'll have more confidence. You build your capacity to handle the unexpected, which minimizes stress.

You meet your goals and fulfill your potential

Proactivity gives you a map for progress; reactivity is wandering aimlessly around shiny objects. When you take the initiative, create meaningful goals, and work toward them, you tap into new skills and abilities. You grow, excel in your responsibilities, and build meaningful relationships. You shape your future instead of leaving it to chance.

You prepare for leadership

Proactivity makes you valuable for leading any team. You're focused on getting results in projects and people, and you're invested in building a unified team that excels. It accelerates your path to career advancement.

You solve problems and make better decisions

When you're proactive, you have time to research well, pull new ideas and information together, and then plan and strategize carefully. You grow your problem-solving muscles each time, and you hone your ability to make choices well.

You're happier

When you're proactive, you have more control over the right things. You're prepared to deal with challenges and capture opportunities. You're focused on solutions instead of problems, so your attitude toward everything in life improves. You're living out your values, which is the foundation for true satisfaction. You're growing your career and yourself, and you're making a difference.

Proactivity will help you in every area of your life. When you're in any situation where you need to read the room, you won't be worried about how you're coming across; you'll feel confident, which allows you to make a genuine impact.

How to Make the Switch

If you've always had a more reactive filter through which you view life, it might seem challenging to adopt a new, proactive one. Fortunately, it's mostly a change of mindset—simply deciding that it's worth making the change. Then, make the path easy through small, actionable steps.

First, recognize that you have the power to change your situation. There will always be factors outside of your control, but what you do and how you respond will determine what happens in your future. With a proactive mindset, you'll have the ability to take control and move forward.

Second, decide to trade in your victim mentality for a victor mentality. You can decide that you have the right skills and mindset to work through the stickiest challenges and create new solutions.

Third, realize that change comes from thinking differently. If you try to commit to new behaviors, you're operating from willpower, which is always a limited resource. To act differently, you need to think differently. To think differently, you need to recognize the lenses you're using and replace them with new ones—lenses that give a different perspective.

And fourth, practice updated behaviors:

- Stop putting things off—act early.
- When an issue arises with someone, take the initiative to talk openly with them instead of avoiding it. (We'll talk about how to do that comfortably.)
- Focus on what you can control. There's only one thing you have control of: *you*. Yourself, your actions, your attitudes, and your choices. What can you *not* control? Everything else.
- Be intentional about self-awareness. Become a student of you.
- Protect your mind by minimizing your negative inputs. If the news triggers your victim mentality, turn it off. Be selective about the content and tone of podcasts you listen to and articles you read. Even if they're positive,

too much input from others tends to put them in charge of what you think.

- Do different things or do things differently. Shake things up occasionally.

If you want to learn to read a room, start developing a mindset of proactivity—the belief that it's possible to perform beyond your current abilities. It's the first leg of your three-legged stool and a foundational step that will impact not just your work but every aspect of your life.

CHAPTER 3

Master the Process

It's Worth the Effort

My ability to read the room is the reason I stay home a lot.

Anonymous

Think about walking into a social event, whether it's personal or professional. You enter the room; what are you *feeling*? Do you lean more toward anxiety or toward confidence? Are you comfortable, or do you feel like you've just walked onto a stage where you'll be critiqued? You scan your surroundings quickly to get your bearings—how many people there are, how big the room is and how it's laid out, what the tone of the room is, and who you might engage in conversation.

You might feel self-conscious, wondering what people are thinking of you, if you're dressed appropriately, or whether you fit in. You might be observing people's facial expressions, trying to decide who to connect with. Maybe you feel completely unsettled until you get into a safe conversation with someone—anything besides floundering in the middle of the room alone.

Or maybe you feel energized by the occasion, and you're excited about having a good time and making connections that will be helpful to you in the future. Once you've made a plan, you're ready to jump into conversations. How do you feel? Probably confident and energetic because you're good at conversation and connection.

In both cases, you are trying to read the room with the goal of feeling comfortable and confident, observing and deciding what is needed to make that happen. No one wants to dread going anyplace where people are present but rather look forward to such events.

Here's the good news: it's possible—and it's not that hard. You just need to learn to read a room *accurately*. You'll start by making initial observations, but you'll also need to interpret those observations with care. Wrong assumptions lead to wrong actions, which lead to wrong outcomes. Your confidence will come from your competence.

Types of Rooms, Types of People

We enter and read rooms in a wide variety of environments—from business-oriented networking events to sales meetings with clients to market strategy meetings. It can be training sessions, team building events, one-on-one update sessions, or job interviews before a panel of executives. It even reaches into our personal lives, such as when we enter our kitchen and see a broken cookie jar and three tiny humans pointing at each other.

Every room is unique from any other room, but they all have one thing in common: *there are people in the room*.

When we enter any room, we want to figure out what's going on. There might be a few details of the environment to consider, but reading the room means reading the people in that room. Even though they're all individuals, there are a number of roles we need to consider to accurately assess the dynamics of any situation:

- *Leaders and followers*: managers and supervisors as well as those who prefer to take direction and follow instructions.
- *Creative thinkers and analytical thinkers*: those who are "idea people" and those who are more linear and logical (and know how to organize those ideas).
- *Veterans and new hires*: people who have been in their career for decades as well as recent college graduates.
- *Customer-facing and support staff*: those who interact with clients and those who work behind the scenes.
- *Remote workers and office-based employees*: people whose environments are each determined by the nature of their responsibilities.
- *Goal setters and problem solvers*: those who excel at planning and those who excel at solving.
- *Introverts and extroverts*: quiet, deep thinkers and outgoing, fast thinkers.

Let's take that last category as an example.

Extroverts tend to recharge their energy when they're interacting with other people and get drained when they're alone. Introverts are the opposite—recharging while alone so they can function well in groups. Extroverts think by talking, while introverts think by listening. Extroverts think quickly, while introverts think deeply.

When reading a room, you'll find about an equal number of both temperaments. The introverts aren't usually shy (that's a different issue), and the extroverts aren't always extra-talkative. The most obvious difference is that an extrovert will share ideas as they come to mind, before those ideas are fully formed. They're putting them out there and shaping them with others. Introverts won't share their thoughts until they've had time to process them alone. Once they've clarified their thinking, they're more than willing to talk about their ideas.

Here's another example. In the past, there has been a lot of discussion of "right-brained people" and "left-brained people." The research is still inconclusive as to how legitimate that categorization is, but the basic idea is worth considering. Basically, it's about the differences between what happens in the left hemisphere of the brain versus the right hemisphere. The idea is that while people use their entire brain, they favor one side over the other, just like they're either right- or left-handed.

People who are considered "left-brained" are more analytical. They're into facts and figures, and data are their friend. People who are "right-brained" are more creative, operating from feelings and intuition. Put those two people together in a conversation, and they'll be interested in different things. If you're more creative, your perspectives on any topic won't be nearly as interesting to a person who is more analytical. To stay connected, you'll want to explore the middle ground and learn from each other.

This concept also impacts the way a person reads a room:

- Left-brained people pay attention to the overall tone of the room, while right-brained people look at specific things in the room.
- Left-brained people figure things out step-by-step, while right-brained people trust their intuition to understand what's going on.
- Left-brained people like order, while right-brained people are more flexible about what's happening.

- Left-brained people look for facts and evidence, while right-brained people look for experiences and emotions.
- Left-brained people focus on their purpose for being in the room, while right-brained people look for things that are inspiring.
- Left-brained people see a social event as a challenge that needs a solution, while right-brained people see it as a story with different characters.
- Left-brained people are linear, taking things in logical order. Right-brained people look for connections between the various things happening around them.

You don't have to memorize all the details of each different type of room and person. As you're reading rooms, just be aware of the differences. It can actually make your journey easier because it gives you something to explore!

Feeling Comfortable in a Room—The Myths

One of the biggest upsides of developing these skills is *confidence*. With so many benefits to knowing how to read a room and just as many downsides when we don't, it makes sense that we would want to learn—right? So why don't we? What gets in the way?

Part of it centers on some simple myths we just assume are true but need to be challenged. Here are the six most common myths:

1. *If I'm going to be comfortable in a room, I need to be an extrovert.*

   Extroverts often have confidence in social situations because they're good at talking. That's not always a sweet spot for introverts, but they excel at listening. Extroverts typically feed off the energy of a larger group, and introverts shine when they're able to engage in one or two deeper conversations.

It's not a matter of which temperament is best in a social situation; each has different strengths, approaches, and unique ways of interacting. When working within their strengths, both can be completely confident in any situation.

2. *Feeling comfortable in social situations shows that I'm popular.*

   In many cases, the most popular, approached people in the room struggle the most with confidence. The ones who stand in the shadows are often the most comfortable because they've accepted who they are and operate in their areas of strength. They enjoy socializing on their own terms and have no desire to be the focus of the room.

3. *When I'm comfortable in a social situation, I'll be constantly interacting.*

   That might be true for some extroverts, but even they need to catch their breath occasionally. The more outgoing a person is, the more interaction they enjoy. Those who are on the quiet side do more than just converse; they take time to simply observe what's happening around them and listen and process deeply within the conversations they do have, and they aren't afraid to step out for a break when they need it.

4. *Feeling comfortable at a social event is a natural trait; either I have it or I don't.*

   Everything we do for the first time is awkward and uncomfortable. Our skills improve as we keep growing and practicing. Reading a room gets easier as we master a simple framework (which we'll discuss in later chapters).

5. *If I am genuinely comfortable in a room, I'll never get nervous or anxious.*

   When the stakes are high, almost everyone gets nervous. When the stakes are low . . . not so much. Just watch the tryouts for talent shows like *American Idol*; even the best performers show high anxiety because it's the biggest platform they've ever been on.

   If we could get rid of all stress, we'd never accomplish anything. Stress is a normal part of life. If we don't control it, it's debilitating. If we manage it well, it gives us energy for high performance.

6. *I'm a people pleaser, so I'll never get away from the pressure to please in any room.*

   In a group setting, people pleasers focus on how they're coming across. They've subconsciously learned how to craft an image of confidence that's artificial, trying to get people to like them. Unfortunately, it might help them get the attention they're looking for, but they know that people aren't responding to who they really are—only the image they're projecting. The positive responses feel hollow because they're based on fantasy instead of reality.

Confidence Inside and Out

One of the most common ways people try to overcome a lack of confidence is to "fake it till you make it." That approach seems logical since confident people seem to get all the attention and breaks and opportunities. Studies have shown that people are perceived as more attractive when they exude confidence.[1] So, if we want to be successful in any situation, it's tempting to work extra hard on looking confident—even if we're not.

If that's the path we take to success, we'll ultimately fail. Pretending to be confident reinforces the fact that we're *not* feeling confident. Nothing has changed on the inside. Plus, pretending to be something we're not is exhausting. We never get to relax and be ourselves because we're so busy performing.

Can you become confident instead of just pretending? Absolutely! It can become your reality, but only when you change your mindset. And that means giving up on *appearing* confident to begin the journey of *becoming* confident.

It's an inside-out job.

That's why you picked up this book. You want to gain the confidence you need in every area of life, but you want it to be genuine. In part 2, we'll work through the simple, step-by-step framework. Those steps apply to everyone, no matter what your temperament or background.

Confidence comes from competence. Learn the right skills and you'll be ready for any situation. You'll know what to look for, and you'll feel confident because you've been trained. You won't have to guess; you'll apply what you know, regardless of the environment.

Imagine never having to worry about what you'll be facing when you enter any room. Wouldn't it be great to lose that anxiety so you can relate to others with excellence? It can make a huge difference for you as well as the people you encounter.

But Wait . . . There's More!

So far, we've focused on how we *feel* when we enter any room. That's the perfect place to start because, for most people, it's the biggest pain point. We're not worried about making a big difference yet; we're more concerned with survival and feeling comfortable and anxiety-free no matter what's happening around us. That's why confidence is relevant to study and is a critical component of success. The more confident we feel, the freer we'll be to move forward.

Twentieth-century psychologist Abraham Maslow is famous for theorizing his hierarchy of human needs, which suggests that there are five levels of needs we all have:

1. Basic physiological needs (food, water, shelter, sleep)
2. Safety and security needs (health, employment, property, family)
3. Love and belonging needs (relationships, sense of connection, intimacy)
4. Esteem needs (confidence, unique identity, respect of others)
5. Self-actualization needs (reaching inner potential and finding personal fulfillment, meaning, and purpose)[2]

These needs progress in order: a person lost in the woods at night won't be as concerned about what others think of them.

In social situations, this means that we might want to make a difference for others in the room, but if we don't feel confident, it'll be tough to make that happen. That's why we commit to learning and mastering the process we'll be covering.

There's one more perspective that's important if we're going to be successful at leading a room: *making sure we see people accurately*. When we meet someone, it's easy to watch them and decide what their motives are without checking to see if we're right. It's like coming across a dog that looks friendly but turns out to be mean. It's risky to believe our first impressions, and it gets in the way of real relationships.

How can we learn to see (read) people accurately instead of guessing? Keep reading . . .

CHAPTER 4

Master Your Perceptions

You Can Learn to See Others Accurately

> Sometimes I listen to a stranger's conversation and mentally give my opinion.
>
> Unknown

I arrived early for my meeting, entering the downtown high-rise as the crowd began to arrive. The massive glass and steel lobby vibrated with businesspeople rushing to get to their offices on time. They shot through multiple doors and beelined for the turnstiles, leveling their badges over the security sensors to gain access. Then they deftly crisscrossed each other's paths, heading for the proper elevators to lift them to their destinations.

No one talked to each other; they followed the same pattern they followed every day. It was as if there were unspoken rules that applied. Nobody was trying to impress anybody else, and nobody was communicating. Everyone was focused on getting to their offices, where the real work would happen. It was quiet chaos and one of those necessities of life everyone accepts in order to get paid.

It reminded me of the times as a kid when I'd stir up an ant hill with a stick, just to see them swarm.

Once I had reached the right elevator, I stood with others in a silent cluster until the doors opened. Then we all squeezed inside, turned, and faced forward. I was shoulder to shoulder with strangers in a mahogany-paneled box that would take us where we needed to be.

Then, as the doors were closing, a young man jumped in at the last second, forcing the doors to reopen briefly. He was in the center at the front of the group but didn't turn around. He directly faced everyone else, then said, "Good morning!" He smiled and tried to make eye contact. Nobody else said a word, but you could feel the temperature rising. He'd broken the rules. In a swarm of anonymity, he had tried to inject a human moment. Plus, he remained facing the wrong way the whole time, until he got off.

A few floors later I reached my destination, and several others exited with me. I walked behind them as they discussed what had happened—now that they were out of the elevator and talking was "allowed." "Well, that was creepy," one person said. "For sure," said another. "What was he trying to do?" "Can you imagine having to work with someone like that?"

On the way home later that day, I reflected on the incident. Yes, it was awkward. At the very least, it was interesting. But the conversation I'd eavesdropped on was even more telling. Here were people who didn't know this person or anything about him, determining that they didn't like him. They hadn't talked to him or asked him any questions; they simply observed something and made a judgment about his character.

And that became their truth.

Unconscious Bias

We all do that, don't we? When we meet someone, we take in data about their looks, their mannerisms, and their words and immediately decide how we feel about them. We think we're objective and unbiased, but we "profile" them based on first impressions. Often, it's because something they said or did reminds us of someone else, so we assume they're just like that person. If we like that other person from our past, we tend to feel good toward this new person. If they remind us of a person we've struggled with, we feel negative from the start.

For example, say you're assigned to a project team at work with people you don't know. One of them is twenty years older than you and reminds you of your tech-challenged grandfather. The other is twenty years younger than you and reminds you of a reckless sorority sister you had in college. You don't know anything about them—but immediately, you make assumptions. Though you haven't spoken to either of them, you already hold a bias about them with no basis in fact.

Later, we might talk with that new person and change our original perception. But until we have those initial conversations and encounters, we only have first impressions—and it's human nature to believe those impressions are true.

Is it fair to have those first impressions? Not really, because we're making assumptions without knowing anything about the person. But it's reality. It's where we start. The key isn't to try turning off those first impressions; it's about recognizing that they're there, then going deeper and being intentional about learning more so we see them as the person they really are.

In a laboratory, researchers begin by shaping a hypothesis, saying "I'm making an assumption that X is true." It's kind of like their "best guess" based on their observations. Then they study everything they can to see if their observations are true or not. If the evidence doesn't support their hypothesis, they've discovered that it isn't true—and they revise the hypothesis. They keep testing against the revised hypothesis to see if it's accurate. They had no expectation that their original hypothesis was true; it was just a place to start on a journey to discover what's real.

Testing the Truth

Where do our first impressions come from? And why can five different people have five different first impressions when they encounter the same person? The difference in perspective comes from the filters those five people use when they're viewing something.

We all believe that we see people accurately. After all, we're looking right at that person, and what we assume is true about them seems obvious. But if you look at the same person and assume something different than I do, your conclusions don't make sense to me. I think you're wrong, and you think I'm wrong. What makes the difference?

We're each the product of a whole bunch of things that have shaped us:

- *Our background*: how and where we were brought up and our life experiences
- *Our culture*: the people we were brought up around—their collective beliefs, values, and ways of doing things
- *Our education*: the things we've learned, whether formally or informally, that have given us the tools we use for living
- *Our language*: the words and speech patterns we use to communicate
- *Our experience*: the collection of events and situations we've lived through

We don't question these things; we simply accept them as true. Add them all up, and they make the filters we use to view everything and everyone we meet.

No one has the same combination of filters as anyone else, which is why we all see things differently.

Let's say that you and I have just met virtually, and I don't know where you live. You say, "It's supposed to be really cold this week." Since I live in Southern California, I picture stepping outside on my patio where the temperature might be forty degrees *above* zero (Fahrenheit), while you're picturing forty degrees *below* zero. If you know I'm using the term "cold" to describe my forty-degree temperature, you'll think I'm crazy. Or, if you say it's going to be windy, you'll post a picture on social media of trees bending in a hurricane—while I post a picture of a lawn chair that blew over and a caption saying, "We will rebuild."

Most people never consider the impact of their filters. They believe they're seeing something correctly, so the other person must be seeing it incorrectly.

The solution is simple: instead of using our first impressions to critique others, we can use them to test for truth. Those first impressions can be triggers to search for the other person's filters. How? We start with a hypothesis, then go on a quest to see if it's accurate. As new data appears, we change our hypothesis. The result? We can have real relationships with people who are different from us.

Let's go back to our example. Our hypothesis/first impression with the older worker: *this person is too old to be any good with technology*.

Our search for data:

- "So, tell me your story."
- "What kinds of jobs have you had before coming here?"

- "Looks like this project has a lot of tech requirements. I'm pretty good with tech stuff—what about you?"
- "What are you looking forward to the most on this project?"

Our hypothesis/first impression with the younger worker: *this person is too young and experienced to take this project seriously*.

Our search for data:

- "So, what's your background before coming to this company?"
- "What do you like best about working here?"
- "Why do you think they picked you for this project? For me, I think it's because I'm pretty good with tech stuff. What's your sweet spot?"
- "Have you worked on this type of project before?"

Remember, it's OK to have an initial bias in our first impression, as long as we know it's just a starting place. Our exploration might reinforce that impression, or it might need to be revised. It's a hypothesis—and our goal is to look for truth beyond our initial assumptions.

Being intentional about overcoming our unconscious biases is the foundational skill for reading any room accurately. It's tempting to walk into a new situation and size people up just by looking at them. It's like we're triaging the room to decide who we like, who we don't like, and what each person is really like based on their appearance and mannerisms. We tell ourselves a story about each person, creating a mental map of the room. It's as if we list everyone's name on a cocktail napkin and add a descriptive phrase about each one.

That's dangerous because we assume those phrases are true—and we'll likely be wrong. When we're wrong, our decisions to relate to them (or not) are based on bad information.

We'd set ourselves up for greater success if we captured those first impressions and realized they were only a place to start. Like a good scientist, we'd now have a personal agenda for the event: to test our hypotheses as we talk to people in the room. We wouldn't have to worry about how we're coming across or try to impress them. We'd be focused on finding out who they are, and we would have real things to talk about.

That doesn't mean we'll end up as best friends with everyone. Some of our impressions will be reinforced, and others will change. We'll be more drawn to some people when we discover their filters and where they come from, and we'll be less drawn to others. That's OK because this isn't about people-pleasing. It's about learning who people are without feeling like we have to fix them.

Let Them Be

When we feel the need to change other people, we'll be frustrated. The more we learn to accept people as they are, the more relaxed we'll be. That doesn't mean they'll never irritate us. Even our best friends do that occasionally, and we stick with them anyway.

In a work setting, we all have to work with people who are different from us—some positively, some negatively. It's normal to let a bad attitude simmer without saying anything, playing along to keep our jobs while thinking they're crazy. But it's exhausting to pretend all the time. It takes a lot of energy, and we harbor resentment.

It's a lot easier to get curious, seek to understand them, and let them be who they are.

Whenever we think, *I'll never be happy until that other person changes*, we're being reactive instead of proactive and are setting ourselves up for failure. We've also given away our own happiness to the behavior of others.

Trying to change other people is an exercise in futility. Think how hard it is to change ourselves; what makes us think it would be any easier to change others? The more we can accept the things we can't control, the more satisfied we'll feel in any situation.

Reading the room goes beyond making assumptions. It's about making the effort to learn the truth. Knowing what's really going on with others allows us to make accurate decisions on how we treat them and work with them. We're not trying to get everyone to like us. Knowing what's true allows us to become confident in who we are so we can relate to others with integrity.

Cross-Cultural Connections

My son's wedding was in Guadalajara, Mexico, a few years ago. Tim met Lucy about six years before that when he was spending a few months working at a Christian conference center and school where she was a student. They started dating and eventually tried to get a visa for her to visit America, but she was repeatedly turned down. So, they built their relationship online for those six years. He visited her a couple of times a year, but she couldn't come to the United States.

When we were two months away from the wedding, my wife and I still hadn't met her. My wife, Diane, didn't want to wait until the ceremony to meet her future daughter-in-law, so she traveled to Mexico to connect with her. Lucy didn't speak English, and she didn't speak Spanish. But they spent several days together and found ways to communicate.

Diane and I tried taking a digital Spanish course to learn the basics. But the phrases they taught—such as "I have been to Chicago" and "Do you like jazz?"—had little to do with typical conversations. When we traveled to Mexico for the wedding, Tim interpreted for us when he was available. But he had a wedding to deal with, so we were pretty much on our own. We knew several of his bilingual friends who were there, and they also made our lives a little easier.

At the reception, we were seated with Lucy's parents, who we'd stayed with the night before. They were wonderful people, and neither of us knew each other's language. We did the best we could, smiling a lot at each other and saying things we hoped would be understood—but it wasn't happening.

Even without words, we found a strong connection with them—not through our words, but through our hearts. We all shared one thing in common: our love for our kids. We had different languages and different cultures, but we all understood the investment we had made that brought us to this day. Years later, Diane and I still need someone to interpret when we connect with them. But we already have that deep connection because of what we have in common (including three grandkids).

It's called *cross-cultural communication*—the process of connecting with someone who is different than we are.

That describes everyone in our lives. They're all unique, and they're all different than we are. If we do it well, we recognize that our whole lives are exercises in cross-cultural communication.

We're naturally drawn to those who are most like us and not interested in those who aren't. When the differences are too great, we engage in cross-cultural *lack of communication*. The less we have in common, the less we try.

The key is to go beyond our first impressions of everyone we meet. We need to recognize our assumptions, then turn them into an initial hypothesis. We test for the truth, revise our hypothesis, then relate to each person based on who they really are.

Everyone has something valuable to contribute. Be the person willing to find out what that is. Engage with them, explore, and do something with it. If everybody else writes someone off, be the person who doesn't. Look past the first impression to see their unique skills and perspective.

Let your unconscious bias become your conscious connection.

More than Check Marks

In the next section, we'll begin the specific process of learning how to read a room with confidence and precision. In these first three chapters, we've built the foundation and have learned:

1. The key perspective for reading a room (growing a proactive mindset)
2. The tangible benefits of a proven process (deciding it's worth the effort)
3. The critical importance of seeing others accurately (growing real relationships)

Before reading further, make sure you've caught a solid vision for your motivation. If you're going to master the art of reading and impacting a room, it won't be by just grabbing a few random tips and tricks and putting them in place. That might impress a few people, but it's not coming from the base of who you are on the inside. Taking an inside-out approach will make all the difference.

Many years ago, when television was in its infancy, the old Zenith Television Corporation had a well-recognized motto: "The quality goes in before the name goes on."[1] It implied that they wouldn't put a television set up for sale until it met their quality standards, and people came to trust the brand. We're not looking for check marks that say we pulled a few things out of a book and put them into practice. We're looking to become the kind of quality people who have the character to make a dent in the world—people with a "brand" others can trust.

Best of all, to do this you don't have to become someone you're not. No matter what your temperament, you get to be yourself. That's your "superpower"—the exact thing that will make you effective. You don't have to compare yourself with anyone else or act like them. You simply need to be *you*. Anytime you try to do what everyone else does, you rob the world of the contribution that only you can make.

Ready for the rest of the ride? I'll see you in the next section!

How to Read a Room (for Confidence)

Years ago, I took my first CPR course. My wife needed to take it each year to maintain her professional certification as a personal fitness trainer, and I decided to tag along. I figured it would be nice to know what to do if someone nearby lost consciousness and their heart stopped, and I could jump in and make a difference. *It's good to be prepared*, I thought.

We "graduated" at the end of the day, and the instructor gave us each a small review card with the process spelled out in case we needed a reminder. I put it in the glove compartment of my car, along with the car registration, instruction manuals, insurance cards, receipts, brochures about local attractions, and a couple of bags of half-eaten snacks.

Even though I ended up attending the course several times, I never got to use what I'd studied. With no application, most of what I learned disappeared. If someone faced a life-threatening event today and I was the only other person around, I wouldn't know what to do (except I think it has something to do with humming "Stayin' Alive" during chest compressions). My first response would be to run to my car and start sifting through all the junk in the glove compartment to find that review card. I'd have to carry it over to the person in need, then lay it on the ground in front of me while I tried to remember how to administer each step. Then I'd have to go back and get my reading glasses . . .

I could spend more time learning other skills as well that would be helpful, but I only have so much time. There is one skill, however, that is priceless for all of us. It's something we've all had practice in because we do it almost daily without even thinking. We have the "reps," but we might not have the training to know how to do it correctly. If we learn how to do it well, it can determine the outcome of every situation we encounter.

What's that essential skill? *Knowing exactly how to read a room.*

We walk into a variety of situations every day and immediately try to see what's happening. Based on what we see, we decide what to do. But if we haven't learned exactly what to look for and how to handle it, we make assumptions that might not be accurate. When we act on inaccurate assumptions, we get bad outcomes—and we lose the ability to make a serious impact in those situations.

Football coach Vince Lombardi said, "Practice does not make perfect. Only perfect practice makes perfect."[1] I could get a sales job where I was encouraged to make one hundred cold calls per day. But if I had never been taught how to make those calls effective, I would just be reinforcing my poor technique.

Now it's time for our game plan. This section will cover the four steps needed to read any room with confidence:

Observe the setting. Discover what's *really* happening in the room. You can get the big picture by observing the whole room with precision and get the small picture by reading people like a book.

Engage with people. Converse with curiosity and purpose. You can learn how to connect and converse with anyone.

Plan your approach. Determine a simple framework for effectiveness by customizing your approach.

Execute your strategy. Take action on your discoveries to impact the room by learning how to work the room.

As we jump in, let me reinforce two facts:

1. You can do this.
2. It's worth the effort.

It doesn't matter if you're an introvert or an extrovert, young or old, experienced or a novice. The steps are simple and sequential. Master them, and you'll be able to respond in the way that is most appropriate for your temperament. You'll gain *confidence*, which benefits you; you'll also gain *competence*, which benefits others. You won't have to become someone you're not; you'll be able to enter every room with the confidence that you know exactly what to do.

Ready to start the journey? Let's take the first step together.

CHAPTER 5

Observe the Setting, Part 1

Get the Big Picture

When you really pay attention, everything is your teacher.

Unknown

Most people have tunnel vision when they first enter a room. They're not proactively thinking about the big picture but rather focusing on the first thing that captures their attention, which is usually the biggest threat or the most exciting thing happening. Someone who's uncomfortable will notice the things that reinforce their uncertainty and wonder how they'll navigate them. Someone who's more confident will be looking for the best opportunity to make something happen.

If we're going to read any room effectively, we need to learn how to avoid this tunnel vision. Instead, we need to learn how to step back and focus on the big picture before focusing on the details.

Start by Becoming Invisible

It might seem unnatural to explore the big picture when you first walk into a room. A lot of things are going on, and you'll probably default to noticing what's right in front of you. It might be a person you recognize or a group of people talking who you wouldn't expect to be connected with each other. It could be what's on the food table, especially if it's an unusual display. Or someone might come over to talk to you.

At the same time, you might be wondering how you're coming across—what others are thinking about you, if they're silently critiquing you, or if they notice that you're uncomfortable in a crowd. (Spoiler alert: they're probably not thinking about you at all. If they are, they're probably just wondering what you're thinking about them.)

When any of that happens, you've short-circuited your ability to read the room. You've skipped the important first step of exploring, and you've moved straight into the second step of engaging. You can't get the big picture if you're engaged only in the small picture. It's sometimes called "situational awareness"—being aware of who's in the room, what the setting is, and how people are interacting. That provides the foundation for figuring out your game plan for that room.

You can't read the room when you're talking. Observing doesn't take long, and it's simple and nonthreatening. If you hear words coming out of your mouth as soon as you walk in, it's a sign that you skipped the first step.

Observing would be a lot easier if you could watch from an adjoining room, looking through a one-way mirror. Obviously, that's usually not an option. But it's easy to read the room when you're not participating in the dynamics of the room. You can be totally objective because you don't have the distractions of interaction. You can simply observe, noticing details such as:

- Body language. Observe people's posture and facial expressions. Do people look relaxed or tense?
- Group dynamics. Who is connecting with who? Are small groups forming? How many people are standing alone?
- Tone. Do the interactions look energetic or subdued?
- Environment. How is the layout impacting conversations? Are people in small groups or spread out? Notice the lighting, music, and other noises in the room; what kind of mood do they provide?
- Emotional climate. Does the room feel tense or upbeat?
- Dominant personalities. Who seem like the most influential people in the room?

When you've had a chance to understand what's happening in the room as a whole, you'll find it a lot easier to become part of it. You won't just be trying to make every conversation work; you'll be able to "work" the room based on your clear understanding of the dynamics you've observed.

By observing first, you'll have a foundation for more satisfying conversations. You'll enjoy connecting more, and people will enjoy being with you more. You won't just be pretending to be comfortable; you'll *be* comfortable. It takes off the pressure of having to be more outgoing and gregarious than you are because you don't have to perform. You can be completely yourself, which is highly attractive to others.

A big reason for reading the room is so we can connect with each other and share the same experience. That connectedness is tied to a sense of happiness and belonging. Getting the big picture at the beginning prepares you to be yourself in conversation because you're able to focus outward instead of just inward.

"OK," you say. "I get it. But there's not a one-way mirror in most of the rooms I have to enter. I have to show up and walk in. How can I stay invisible enough to observe when there's so much going on?"

Fair question. Here are a few ideas to consider.

Start outside

Find a position outside the room that's not too obvious where you can watch people approach the meeting room door. Notice their facial expressions and body language before they go in. I've discovered that the expressions and posture of almost half of the people entering a room have the scent of insecurity, and they take a deep breath before opening the door. Immediately, a broad smile crosses their face, their posture improves, and they plow into the room with energy and enthusiasm that seems to have appeared out of nowhere. It's like they flipped the "gregarious" switch as they moved into action.

We'll learn later about why we can't make a lot of assumptions about people with just one or two behaviors we observe. But in general, do your initial observing outside the room to get a sense of how people are feeling just before they enter.

Tip: if it's tough to observe unobtrusively without people noticing you and talking to you, sit down and put your phone to your ear. You don't have to talk; it will just keep people from engaging with you as easily.

Move inside with a plan

After you've gotten a sense of how people behave just before entering a situation, it's time to go into the room with a sense of mission. Avoid conversation (for now) and take in as much data as you can to get the big picture.

It doesn't matter what room you're entering. You'll just tailor the approach to the situation.

- If you're attending a company conference, use the same approach at any social event as described below.

- If you're going into a job interview, read the room ahead of time by doing your research. Find out everything you can about the company, the person you'll be working for, the person you'll have the initial interview with (background, expertise, interests, experience, etc.), and anything else you can discover. When you arrive, jump into observation mode as soon as you enter the building, watching people's attitudes, posture, and interactions. Eavesdrop on their conversations just enough to get a sense of what the work environment is like. When you walk into the interview, quickly look around and observe everything you can that will give you hints about that person's priorities and interests.
- If you're attending a weekly meeting for your department, ask for the agenda ahead of time and study it. You'll probably be the only one who reads the agenda, so it will give you an edge in the conversation.
- If you're making a pitch to a client, do the same research you would for a job interview. See if you can discover who else they've worked with, then connect with them to learn about the client's priorities.
- If you're making a speech, don't just prepare your presentation. Put just as much time into knowing who will be there and what their priorities, interests, and needs are as you put into the topic.
- If you're in a weekly one-on-one meeting with your boss, keep curious in the days before about what they're involved in—what's stressing them, what big priorities they are focused on this week, and what's on their plate that concerns them. Reading the room in that way gives you an advantage because you can prepare to offer empathy and even solutions for the issues they're facing.
- In a larger meeting, do everything you can to observe as much as you can from the start. Enter the room with

the intent to observe but stay in motion. If someone calls you over, just keep moving and say, “Hey, great to see you. I’ll be back in a bit.” It keeps you from having to stop and chat just because someone asked until you’re ready. The extra advantage is that in this setting, most people are simply being social and trying to make conversation. They’re inviting you to join their group but probably won’t even remember if you never make it back to them. That way you can choose another time to connect if you’d like later in the event.

- Be intentional about making observations, noticing everything happening around you with precision. Use your gut to sense what’s happening in the environment. Is it formal or informal? How are people dressed? Does it feel like a positive environment or a negative one?
- Keep an eye on conversations that are ending. Watch the facial expression of each person as they walk away to see if they reflect satisfaction at the connection or relief that it’s over.
- Look for positive things happening in the room. If you see a senior executive in a group conversation, see if they’re smiling. Notice who they’re with; are they with people at the same level in the organization as them, or are they engaging with the everyday employees?
- Look for the pecking order. If the boss walks in the room, watch everyone’s posture and facial expressions to get a sense of how they feel about them.
- Look for people who are talking but not listening and listening but rarely talking.

You don’t have to remember everything you see. Just stay focused on taking in data at this point and avoiding conversations. It won’t take long; just make sure it happens.

What's for Breakfast?

If there's a food table, it's natural to visit it quickly to see what's available. As much as you can, try to avoid grabbing a plate until you've made your initial observations about the room.

Once you decide you're ready to visit that table, try not to start conversations while filling your plate. You can't shake hands, and it's tough to have a good connection when you're wandering past different sides of the table. Fill your plate quickly before moving toward an individual or group you'd like to connect with.

Pro tip: if you'll be moving to a table to eat after getting your food, go ahead and fill your plate. If you'll be standing while talking to others, stick with finger foods at first so you don't have to negotiate holding a plate and fork while conversing. You're trying to reduce conversational friction as much as possible, so save the full meal until after you've made connections.

Go with Your Gut

It shouldn't take long to make these initial observations. Remember, you're not getting into minute detail yet. You're trying to stand back and get the big picture of what's going on. It's something most people never even consider, so it will put you at a huge advantage as you participate in the event. You took the time to be curious, and you'll feel a whole different level of confidence because you've been paying attention. That will inform your choices going forward.

Find a couple of minutes as soon as possible to do a quick mental review of what you've seen, or even jot down a few notes. List them as a single paragraph or bullet points—an overall impression of the dynamics. It's simply a statement of how you see the big picture. It doesn't have to be perfect, and it definitely won't be absolutely accurate. You're forming your initial hypothesis, which you know will probably change as you get more information. At the least, you'll be ready to test that hypothesis by moving into the second part of observing the setting: *getting the small picture*.

CHAPTER 6

Observe the Setting, Part 2

Get the Small Picture

> It was impossible to get a conversation going; everybody was talking too much.
>
> Yogi Berra

My usual coffee shop was crowded, but I found a table near a window to get some writing done. After getting settled and putting in my noise-canceling earbuds, I did a quick scan of the room. It's become a habit since I've been writing about "reading the room," and it's always interesting to get a sense of what's happening when I can't hear the conversations.

The big picture seemed pretty normal and included some of the regulars who took the same seats every day. Some people were relaxed and smiling and enjoying their conversation. Others had their laptops open and papers spread out as they worked on various projects, and one man was talking to his screen, obviously on a video call (I hope). The tables along a wall of unshaded windows were empty because of the bright morning sun. Overall, it was a comfortable, drama-free setting—which is why people were showing up there.

There was one exception at a couple of tables in the middle of the room. A young couple sat on one side of the first table, across from a high-energy salesperson. The couple's two young boys were at the table behind them, playing games on a couple of tablets.

As I couldn't hear the conversation, I could only watch their body language and facial expressions. It was a perfect opportunity for me to go to the next level of observation and study the "small picture"—individual people in the room instead of the whole room.

They were already at their table when I arrived and were still going when I left two hours later. The salesperson talked nonstop, while the couple sat and stared at him, almost expressionless. It looked like they were listening intently because their eye contact was steady. The man had a furrowed brow the whole time, as if concerned about something. The woman simply had a blank stare that almost never changed. All three had matching sheets of paper in front of them, which were filled with data and numbers, and the salesperson kept scribbling numbers quickly, circling and underlining and drawing arrows to make his point.

Once in a while, the salesperson told what must have been a funny story, because the couple laughed politely. I noticed that they laughed with their mouths, but their eyes didn't move. I've learned that real smiles and laughter always make eyes crinkle—which is a quick way to tell if it's a real reaction or fake. Theirs didn't. Plus, their reaction ended quickly instead of tapering off slowly, dropping at once back to their blank stares.

I don't know what the conversation was about or what was being presented. But even without hearing a word, I could sense what the couple was feeling. I wasn't just observing; I was identifying with their emotions. I've had the same feelings over the years in timeshare presentations, certain multilevel opportunities, and with home improvement people trying to sell a high-dollar upgrade that I didn't want. They had such logical, persuasive presentations that it was tough to think clearly in the moment. All I wanted to do was get away, but I didn't know how to do it graciously.

The fascinating part was that I could tell exactly what was happening without hearing a word. I could do the same thing with everyone else in the room if I wanted. It wouldn't be totally accurate, but adding the "small picture" to the "big picture" would enable me to read the room more accurately.

Why? Because we're human. We know what we feel as humans in different situations, which makes it possible to spot it in others. Even without words, we can sense what's happening with the people around us.

Hearing What's Not Spoken

Someone said that the best way to take the temperature of the room is to take the temperature of the people in the room. In the first level of observing the setting, we looked at the room as a whole. In this second step, we focus on individuals. We're not engaging with them yet or even listening to their words in most cases; we're gathering data from watching their nonverbal cues.

This is a tricky concept because we can watch someone make a gesture or a facial expression and make assumptions about them—but be completely wrong.

Years ago, I was teaching a class of young adults at our church on a particular Sunday. One woman I knew listened intently but had a nasty scowl on her face the entire time I was talking. She would frown deeply and often look down a bit while shaking her head back and forth as if to say, "Nope. I'm not buying it."

It was tough to keep going with someone who was being so negative. I forged ahead, afraid that everyone else might be feeling the same but not showing it. The session felt like it would never end, and I was trying to stay positive while being critiqued so negatively.

Finally, the session ended. I had to find out what was going on, so I approached her. "Hey, I just needed to check. It seemed like you were struggling with some of the things I was talking about. Is that accurate?"

She looked shocked. "Not at all," she said. "I thought it was amazing! There were so many ideas I hadn't considered, and I was just taking it all in."

"Really?" I said. "You were frowning the whole time and shaking your head like you were disagreeing."

"I had no idea," she said. "I know that when I'm really concentrating, I scrunch up my face to pay attention—and I've been told it looks kind of menacing." As for shaking her head, she had developed a habit of shaking her head back and forth whenever she heard new information, almost as if to say, "I can't believe I've never thought of that."

If I hadn't asked, I would never have known and might have gone on to feel intimidated anytime she was in one of my presentations.

Nonverbal communication can tell us a lot, but it's not as foolproof as we've been led to believe.

When I started researching nonverbal communication for this chapter, I scanned different popular books, articles, and research studies on understanding body language. Each one promised the reader could become wildly successful in all their relationships if they knew how to "read" the body language of other people. The books were filled with static images of people demonstrating various facial expressions, gestures, eye movements, and postures, describing exactly what each one meant.

It all started with a study done by Dr. Alfred Mehrabian, a university professor who wrote an article some forty years ago that has been quoted—and misquoted—ever since. He's reported to have said that 7 percent of our communication comes through the words we say, 38 percent comes through our tone of voice, and 55 percent comes through our body language. If only such a tiny fraction of understanding comes through words, it would make sense to become an expert in body language.

The problem is this is taking what he said completely out of context, even though it's still cited as truth today. Communication coach Nick Morgan summarizes Mehrabian's actual teaching simply: "We get most of our clues of the emotional intent behind people's words from nonverbal sources. And when the two are in conflict, we believe the nonverbal every time."[1]

The sources I consulted made confident claims about different nonverbal cues, implying that we can know exactly what a person is thinking and feeling when they display them. Examples include things like:

- When people look directly at you, they're engaged. If they look away they're either bored, disinterested, or lying.
- If they look down, they're nervous.
- If they blink more than usual, they're either stressed or dishonest (especially if they're also touching their face).
- If they look upward and to the right, they're lying. If they look upward and to the left, they're telling the truth.
- Their feet are pointing toward what they want. If pointed toward you, they're engaged. If pointed toward the door, they want to escape.

While those conclusions might be true, the same movements could also imply other things. For instance, whenever I see someone with their arms crossed in one of my seminars, it may be natural to assume they're resistant or defensive—but most of the time, they're just cold.

It's dangerous to make assumptions about a person based on a single gesture or facial expression. Instead, we must look for what author Gerard Nierenberg calls "gesture clusters"—the combination of multiple gestures—to get a complete picture.[2]

We wouldn't make assumptions about what a book is about simply by reading one word. In the same way, we can't read a person based on a single gesture. "Each gesture a person makes is like a single word in a paragraph," Nierenberg writes. "Words must be structured into units, or 'sentences' which express complete thoughts." He suggests that using gesture clusters is like listening to someone speak an entire sentence instead of a single word to discover their meaning.[3]

When we're reading a book, we read a bunch of words together. When we're reading a person, we need to take into account many gestures and facial expressions to learn what they're thinking instead of assuming that a single expression is the whole truth.

What's New in Body Language Research?

As I started reading those books and articles on body language, I found myself overwhelmed with the number of tiny details I would apparently have to memorize to read people well. Those sources guaranteed success in relationships, but only if I mastered those minute details.

At the same time, most of them had the same information about what each gesture or expression meant. Some of the books were decades old while others were much more recent—but their findings were surprisingly similar. I thought, *Isn't there anything new?* I wondered if people have used the same body language throughout generations. Did a raised eyebrow mean the same thing in the 1800s as it does today?

Rather than reproduce the same content as the popular books, I decided to explore more current research studies to see what we can learn that's simple and applicable. Here's what I found to be the most recent information in each of the major categories.

Body language

As mentioned earlier, we need both words and body language to know what a person is thinking. But if there's a disconnect, body language usually wins. People can try to use their words and tone of voice to convince us of something, but body language is harder to fake.

Television dramas lead us to believe that people who are lying will appear nervous. In reality, there's no evidence of that. People telling the truth can be just as nervous, depending on the situation. Both might display signs of anxiety, but it doesn't confirm who's honest and who's not.

In that case, their words might give them away. When people are lying, they try to keep things simple and without a lot of detail. They know if they say too much, it will be harder to remember exactly what they said later. Truth-tellers are usually more up-front and willing to provide detailed information, knowing they'll be OK if someone checks those details. (That's why Mark Twain said, "If you tell the truth, you don't have to remember anything."[4])

In a group setting, a confident person tends to stand up straighter and hold their head higher. They use larger gestures when talking. A less confident person tends to slouch and drop their head. When someone is upset or angry, their whole body tenses up.

Recognizing the impact of body language is valuable in how we function in any room. In a job interview, for instance, it's important to know how to answer questions accurately and to dress professionally. But if you don't come across as confident, you probably won't get hired.

That's a new wrinkle for younger people who have been brought up communicating largely on digital devices instead of face-to-face. Many haven't had the years of practice with in-person conversations, so their body language gives away their lack of experience.

Bottom line: understanding the basics of body language is worth the effort—not just to read a room but to know how to stand out in that room.

Facial expressions

The primary way we show what we're feeling and discern what others are feeling is through facial expressions. When COVID-19 hit, everyone wore masks—and suddenly we could only see people's eyes.

One of the things that suffered most was empathy—the ability to sense another person's emotions and to imagine what they might be thinking and feeling. We'll talk more about empathy in chapter 17, but the point here is that facial expressions are the primary way empathy occurs. Cover them with a mask, and it's a lot tougher.

A recent article surveying earlier body language books found studies that identified anywhere from twenty thousand to two hundred and fifty thousand different facial expressions. Thankfully, we don't need to distinguish that many nuances of expression.[5]

In fact, the most interesting finding in this article is that no matter what culture people are part of, they show the same facial muscle expressions around the same emotions. We might think expressions are learned from the environment a person grew up in, but they seem to be biologically innate. People who are blind from birth use the same facial expressions when feeling the same emotions. If they're happy or become angry, their facial expressions match those of sighted people—even though they've never seen them.

Another finding that's fairly recent talks about microexpressions. When a person has any type of reaction during a conversation, they might choose the facial expression that seems appropriate to give to others. But slow-motion video has found that before this chosen expression appears, there can be a split-second microexpression that shows their genuine reaction before they transition to the chosen one. Most people never notice them, but they can be detected when you know what to look for. Those tiny expressions include things like the slightest smile or frown, minuscule eyebrow movement, or a tiny eye movement to one side.

The lesson? You can memorize what different facial expressions might mean. But it's more valuable to watch for those expressions with intent. Instead of just sensing them, look for them.

Hands and gestures

When I was a teenager, nobody had cell phones, and everyone wore a wristwatch. One of our pranks when at a wedding or social event was to look to see on which wrist someone was wearing their watch, then notice if they were holding their drink in that hand. If they were, we'd ask, "Do you know what time it is?" Frequently, they'd turn their hand toward themselves to check the time and spill their drink on themselves in the process.

If you've ever watched someone speak with absolutely no gesturing, it feels totally unnatural. Usually, it's because someone told them they use their hands too much when they're talking and they've become self-conscious. It feels (and looks) strange because gesturing is such a natural part of conversation.

Gestures are spontaneous hand movements people make while talking, and they're almost always unconscious. They're tough to craft by design because we're too busy talking and can't do both well at the same time. When we're listening to someone talk, we usually notice their gestures slightly below the conscious level. Those gestures help reinforce what they're saying and so are part of how we understand them, but we don't really see them.

It's time to notice. The next time you're in a room full of people having conversations, stay disengaged long enough to intentionally notice people's gestures. Try picking a few people across the room, where you can see their gestures but can't hear what they're saying. Watch the people they're talking to and notice how they gesture when it's their turn to talk. It's fascinating to observe because gestures are usually not on our radar.

Then move closer so you can hear their words as well, and see if the gestures match what they're saying. Since most gesturing is unintentional, it's a great exercise in noticing what most people do. Once you've practiced this, you'll be much more aware of your own gestures when you're talking. (If possible, ask a friend to unobtrusively take a video of you when you're talking to someone in a meeting so you can watch later and see if you're consistent.)

Eyes

Our eyes play a critical role in communication. When people look each other in the eyes, they become more conscious of themselves and the other person. It tends to create focus, and everything around us fades away. After all, we spend most of our day not being looked at. When someone does look at us, it grabs our attention.

Research has shown that people who use direct eye contact are more likely to be believed than those who avert their gaze. In one study, researchers showed videos of someone making a statement that the viewer probably wouldn't know the accuracy of, such as "Sniffer dogs cannot smell the difference between identical twins." When they looked directly into the camera, the statement was accepted as true much more often than in another video where they looked slightly to the side. If the viewer disagreed with the statement, they were much slower to do so when it had been delivered with direct eye contact.[6]

When people try to force a certain type of eye contact, it usually comes across as contrived and unnatural. In a session I taught on presentation skills, each student prepared and delivered a speech to the rest of the class, who would then critique the presentation.

One student had good content but stared directly at each person for thirty or forty seconds without breaking eye contact. When the critique began, nobody remembered anything he said. All they'd absorbed was the intimidating stare. "Dude, why were you staring at me for so long? That was creepy."

His response: "Really? I remember hearing somewhere that eye contact is important. So, I've worked hard to stare directly into someone's eyes in a conversation and never look away, even for a second."

That's unnatural. The most genuine, comfortable conversations involve a give-and-take of words, gestures, and eye contact. It varies by culture, but Americans tend to keep a gaze for between seven to ten seconds, and a bit longer when they're listening.

The Bottom Line on Body Language

It takes more than words to communicate. Contrary to what many authors have suggested, body language alone doesn't tell the whole story. But when you're learning to read a room, you learn a lot when you notice what a person does even before you hear their words. Then, when you put verbal and nonverbal language together, you'll be much more aware of the whole of their communication.

Pay attention to people's facial expressions, gestures, posture, and body language. Being intentional about observation helps you interpret the feelings and reactions behind their words.

Master the art of observation, and you'll be able to read someone like a book.

CHAPTER 7

Engage with People, Part 1

Connect with Anyone

> Networking is not collecting contacts. Networking is about planting relationships.
>
> Unknown

Ask almost anyone, "What do you do for fun in your spare time?" and you'll rarely hear "networking" as their response.

Most of us know that building relationships plays a significant role in succeeding and advancing in our careers. But there's a stigma about the process that turns most people off. For years, networking events consisted of people who didn't know each other gathering in a room to meet people who might be able to help them in their careers. Everyone pastes on an artificial smile and pretends to be more extroverted than they are, trying to see who can impress each other the most. They exchange business cards and promise to keep in touch, but they never look at those cards again.

That type of networking scenario is almost always ineffective. We do business with people we trust, and it's rare (if not impossible) to trust someone you've just met who is crafting their image to impress you. Everyone compares their comfort level with everyone else's, and they all feel inferior to the overly friendly folks in the room. They leave the event having done what was expected but not finding any real value in it. They do it because they've been told that networking is the secret to getting what they want in their career-related life. They want career success, so they "network" whether they want to or not.

In other words, it all feels fake. It's almost like meeting a bunch of actors who are always in character instead of being themselves. It's interesting, and everyone treats you like their new best friend—but the air seems filled with flattery instead of sincerity.

It doesn't matter if you're an introvert or an extrovert; nobody expects to build real relationships with pretend people. So, how can we get past playing charades and make real connections?

How to Approach People

In the previous two chapters, we did our prep work for reading a room well: *observing*. It doesn't take long to do this first step, but almost everyone neglects it and jumps right into conversation. Taking time to watch what's happening is a huge advantage. It lets you pick up the tone of the room as well as get a sense of strategy for your second step: *engaging*.

In this chapter, we'll talk about how to approach people intentionally. Whether we're in a new setting or a familiar group, we can decide who to talk to instead of gravitating toward the most comfortable person. Then, in the next chapter, we'll discuss how to start a conversation and keep it going. (The same process will apply to digital rooms you've entered, and we'll discuss that in a future chapter. For now, we're talking about in-person events.)

A lot of our hesitation to reach out to others comes from what we tell ourselves. One researcher said, "Although people derive substantial benefits from social connection, they often refrain from talking to strangers because they have pessimistic expectations about how such conversations will go (e.g., they believe they will be rejected or not know what to say)."[1]

As you consider how you're going to approach someone, you'll do well to keep six simple ideas in mind.

First, arrive early. No matter what the event is, you'll feel a lot less stressed if you're prepared. That means you've allowed time to observe what's going on before engaging with people, and then to plan your strategy for who to approach and how you'll make it happen.

Second, focus outward instead of inward. If you're focused on your anxiety and how you're feeling, you'll be worried about how you're coming across instead of how you'll connect. Remind yourself that your purpose isn't to get people to like you; it's to have genuine connections with people you like. With that mindset, you'll be too busy looking for enjoyable conversations to be concerned about people's opinions. (Plus, if you focus on others, they're much more likely to feel positive about you.)

Third, go first—for two reasons:

1. Half the people in any room are waiting for someone to talk to them, and they're feeling the stress of having to approach someone. If you go first and approach them, you just made their whole experience a lot easier—and you probably just became their favorite person in the room.
2. If you wait for someone to approach you to begin a conversation, they're setting the agenda for what you

talk about. If you go first, the initial agenda is in your hands. You set the pace of the conversation as well as the topic.

Fourth, test your assumptions. As you're deciding who to approach, you'll be checking out each person's body language, posture, facial expressions, and so forth. Does it look like they're open to conversation, or do they seem unapproachable? Notice your first impression, then challenge it. Try approaching the person who seems unapproachable and ask a safe, unobtrusive question to get information about something:

(At a company meeting) "Excuse me, I left my agenda at home. Do you happen to have one I could look at for a minute?"

(At a meeting in an unfamiliar location) "Hi! Do you happen to know the WiFi name and password here?"

(At a large event) "I'm trying to find the guest speaker's bio. Do you know where I could find a program or the information table?"

(As a new hire) "I'm new here and just trying to get my bearings. What do you think I need to know that nobody is telling me? Any land mines I should avoid?"

(In line at a coffee shop) "First time here for me . . . what would you suggest?"

By asking for information, you've broken the ice. It's amazing how often someone is ready to engage in conversation, and their closed posture or negative expression could be a protective instinct when they're feeling insecure. If they don't want to talk, you'll discover that without risking rejection. If their response is positive and they seem open, introduce yourself and continue the conversation.

I'm not a big fan of long conversations on airplanes, but I'll usually make a quick comment to a seatmate just as a point of contact. I might comment on the crowdedness of the plane or whether we'll take off on time, or ask about their experience with this particular airline. The way they answer provides just enough information for me to decide what level of engagement would be appropriate. If I feel like connecting a bit, I'll continue the conversation for a while. I usually carry noise-canceling headphones and put them on my lap right away. When the conversation lags a bit (or when I'm ready to take a break), I simply say, "Well, time to get some work done" and put them on while opening my laptop.

I learned the power of headphones on a plane once when I asked the person sitting next to me, "So, are you coming or going?" He didn't say a word, but he looked directly at me with a scowl while he grabbed his headphones and forcibly put them on without ever breaking eye contact. It was his way of saying, "We're not going there." I got the point, and those were the last words I spoke to him for the entire trip.

That's why it's always valuable to make a quick, safe connection to see how the other person responds. You'll know immediately what your options are for continuing. Ask a question, explore a little, then either move forward or exit graciously when necessary.

Fifth, smile. Smiling is a universal nonverbal cue of friendship and connection, so it immediately releases tension for both people. When you smile, it shows that you're approachable, interested, and likable. Most people will smile back, or at least engage with you more quickly than they would otherwise. Make sure your smile is genuine and natural, not exaggerated to make an impression. They'll see through it if it's fake.

Sixth, set realistic expectations. Decide ahead of time what would make the interaction a success for you:

- If you're an introvert at a networking event, don't assume you have to collect thirty business cards because that's what others are doing. You might decide that your goal will be to talk to enough people briefly to find one who you connect with and would like to stay in touch with.

- In a team meeting, make it your objective to ask one good question and contribute one valuable comment. People will remember you for the quality of what you say, not the quantity.
- Assume that everyone you talk to knows something you don't, so set a goal to learn one new thing from each conversation. Your conversations will often be shorter but much more valuable. The next time you connect with that person, bring up the thing you learned from them last time.
- Want to be remembered? Send a quick email of appreciation to one person after each encounter, focused on one thing you observed that person do that made a difference for others in the room.

In other words, don't evaluate your success in any situation based on what someone else does. When you compare yourself with others, you're measuring your own performance against their skillset, not your own.

How to Approach a Group

It can be easier to use the previous tips to try to connect with individuals, because then it's just you and one other person. It might seem safer to try to join an "in-progress" conversation that two or more people are having, but that can be risky. It's possible to "break in," but it needs to be done cautiously—if at all.

For example, they could be having a private conversation about a sensitive issue. If you try to join without knowing what they're discussing, they'll resent the intrusion. It's best to spend more time in observation, looking for the body language and facial expressions that tell you the level or depth of the conversation. If it looks like it's not too serious, always ask permission.

Don't just barge in and start talking. Make it easy for them to turn you down for the moment. Approach cautiously and say something like, "I'm sorry to interrupt, and it looks like you're involved in a conversation. Would this be a good time to join you, or do you want to wave me over when you're done?" If they invite you in, don't talk right away. Listen to catch the flow and build trust, then start with a quick question about something that was said. We've all been in situations where someone just jumped into a conversation and started talking, and it was awkward for everyone. Be the one to recognize that and solve the problem.

Anytime people attend an event where there are both familiar friends and strangers, most people take the safe route and immediately cluster with their friends. It's not bad to hang out with friends, but it eliminates the chance to explore new relationships in the simple ways we've been discussing.

If you want to go on the adventure of meeting new people, don't immediately head for your familiar group because it's the most comfortable. Make a commitment to approach at least one person you don't know to explore a new relationship. Keep it short and simple, then meet with your friends as the reward for completing that initial challenge.

I was at a large company meeting a few years ago where people gathered with their friends at every break. Just before one of those breaks, the moderator said, "We all take these breaks to talk to the people we work with and know the best. But during this break, don't talk to anybody you know. Go find someone you've never talked to and spend the break with them. Get to know each other, and you'll have a new friend."

It was well-meaning, and the motive was good. But when people haven't had training or experience in how to observe others and make those initial contacts, it can be the most threatening part of the event. They'll usually do it because it's expected (or because they've been approached by someone taking the challenge—often an extrovert), but they'll rarely leave with a new friend. They'll just remember how uncomfortable the forced process was.

A better way would be to give them a little coaching before the break. "During this break, before you meet your friends, take two minutes to find someone you don't know and ask this single question: 'If a friend told you they were applying for a job at this company and asked what it was like to work here, what would you say?' That's it. No more than two minutes—then go find your friends."

It's simple, safe, and structured. You could even do it on your own by introducing yourself to one person you don't know and saying, "Can I ask you one quick question?" Pose the question, get their response, talk in more depth if it feels appropriate, and thank them. This allows you to make a connection with another person quickly, and you both separate feeling good about the exchange.

Try It Out

Learning to approach people is a lot simpler and safer than it might sound. It's a skill anyone can learn, and it gets easier with practice. The key is to look beyond yourself and how uncomfortable it feels, where you're worried about how you're coming across and what the other person thinks of you. Shift your focus onto the other person and how you can make the interaction enjoyable for them.

Every day, pick one person to approach and open the conversation. Make a single statement where you find common ground or ask a simple question that's easy for them to answer. Don't do it with the expectation of having a great dialogue (though that might happen). Do it for the experience of taking the initiative and practicing.

For example, several mornings a week I arrive at a Starbucks near my house when they open at 5:00 a.m. The staff all seem to be nice enough, but I don't think any of them are morning people. They rarely talk to each other and don't acknowledge other coworkers when they arrive. Basically, they most likely haven't had their own coffee yet.

Last week, the least energetic person took my order. After I paid, I said, "So, what time did you have to get up this morning to get here?" She perked up a bit and said, "I set my alarm for about 4:30." I followed up with a logical question: "You must not live very far away, right?" She said, "Nope, I'm right down the street."

We bantered back and forth a little, and I wasn't just making small talk with someone who wasn't quite awake; I was asking honest questions that focused on her. It wasn't a manipulative technique, just a human moment that we both appreciated. Since that brief conversation, she at least smiles and says "Good morning" when I come in the door. We still don't talk much, but that little connection made a difference.

The next day, I stopped at the grocery store in the same shopping center to pick up a small container of coffee creamer to take home. The cashier was obviously "morning challenged" as well and didn't give signs of needing or wanting conversation. She took my money and asked routinely, "Do you need a bag for that?" I chuckled at needing a bag for such a small item and said, "No, I think I can manage it." She smiled a little. Then I said, "But do you think I could get someone to help me load it into the car?"

Try it this week and see what happens. Pick someone you're doing business with or meet in any situation and open a conversation. You don't have to keep a conversation going yet—that's in the next chapter. Start with a single comment or question. The more you try it, the easier it will get.

That's what approaching others is all about. It's not about impressing them or collecting business cards. It's about learning to make connections.

Why? Because we're all humans. Maybe we should treat each other that way!

CHAPTER 8

Engage with People, Part 2

Converse with Anyone

> I have more conversations in my head than I do in real life.
>
> Unknown

When a rocket is made ready to launch into space, a lot of things could go wrong. If that happens, the launch team can cancel the process right up until a few seconds before ignition. It's reassuring to know that option is available.

At a certain point, the engines are ignited and it's too late for the team to change their minds. The rocket uses up a huge percentage of its fuel to leave the launch pad and get into orbit. Now the team shifts into a different mode: controlling the details of the flight. From that point on, it's all about making sure the mission is successful.

It sounds a bit like initiating a conversation with a stranger, doesn't it? You spend a lot of time deciding how you're going to begin your "mission," then you take the initial steps to make the connection (as we learned in the last chapter). It takes a lot of energy to walk up to someone and make your first statement. But once you've done it, the conversation has "launched." You don't focus on connecting anymore; it's time to move the conversation forward.

So, what's next?

The Big Power of Small Talk

Someone said that starting a relationship is kind of like two porcupines who fall in love. At first, they're constantly sticking each other and it's painful. But they want to stay close, so they keep trying and gradually learn how to adjust.

That's why it's awkward when someone goes too deep, too fast in the first conversation. Because of that, we open most conversations with something benign like, "Hi, how are you?" If someone's first words are, "Hi! How much money do you make?" or "How much weight have you gained recently?" the conversation ends there.

Deep, personal discussions are appropriate between people who know each other well and have developed a high level of trust. It takes time to develop trust, which is why deep topics feel intrusive if they happen too quickly. Small talk becomes an entry point to a conversation, not an end in itself. We use it to get started, much like an athlete warms up before getting into the real competition.

That's the power of small talk. After you launch a conversation with someone you don't know, small talk is the safest place to begin.

It's common to hear someone complain, "I hate small talk." That's especially true of introverts, who often feel like it's a waste of time. They'd rather spend time talking about things that matter to both people, so they feel irritated if conversations don't progress quickly. It comes from a perception that "Life is short, so let's talk about real issues."

Part of that comes from an inaccurate mindset about small talk. When we look in the dictionary, a typical definition of small talk would be, "Polite conversation about subjects that are ordinary or unimportant, especially at social occasions."[1] If it's unimportant, it's not worth talking about—right?

That definition overlooks the purpose of small talk. We don't make small talk for the purpose of sticking with small talk. It's a launch pad to take a relationship in whatever direction is appropriate. It's a way of building bridges between people, setting them up for deeper conversations around common interests.

Small talk leads to big talk.

At the beginning of a conversation between strangers, small talk allows them to start feeling positively toward each other and ready to have the next level of interaction. It helps them learn about each other so they can find common ground or areas of interest to pursue.

During a conversation, small talk can fill those uncomfortable pauses where no one is speaking. Participants can talk about something less serious until a more meaningful topic pops up. The tolerance we have for silence in deep, intimate relationships would feel painfully awkward in casual conversations.[2]

When any conversation starts to lose energy, small talk provides a way to separate comfortably. If one person simply stopped talking and walked away, it would feel like a blatant rejection.

Starter Topics

A lot of people assume that they need to have a lot of knowledge about a lot of topics to make a conversation work. Fortunately, at this stage, it's not true. Since it's small talk, you want small topics.

That's why people say you shouldn't talk about things like religion or politics in a casual conversation. In the right settings and the right relationships, there could be a place for those subjects. But during small talk, they're almost always out of place. You're simply sticking your toes in the conversational waters to see if you want to go deeper. If a shark lurches at you before you're even ankle-deep, you'll turn and run.

Save the big topics for when the conversation gets big—over time, after trust has been built.

Looking for common ground is appropriate in both small talk and big talk. In initial get-acquainted conversations, ask simple questions to explore the options. Think of the things that both of you experience:

- Find out where they grew up or lived over the years to see if there's any overlap from your own experience.
- Ask what brings them to this event and see if it fits with your reasons.
- If you work for the same company, find out what department and how long they've been there.
- Travel is always a good topic, so find out where they've been.
- The weather is almost too easy to talk about, so only bring it up if it's significant at the moment (unusually hot, cold, windy, and so forth).
- Bring up sports but be careful not to let it take over the discussion if they're a raving fan. Just find out what sports they're interested in, if any.

When they ask, "How are you?" they're not interested in your entire medical history or extended family issues that are stealing your focus. It's tempting to jump into a long story about something in your life, but remember to keep the focus primarily on them. The more they talk about themselves and the less you talk about yourself, the greater the positive impression will be. There will be time for exploring each other's lives once the relationship has grown, but it's risky when you're in the early stages of the relationship.

Your Two Most Powerful Resources in Conversation

When starting conversations with people we've just met, we often feel the need to talk about ourselves and impress them so they'll like us. In reality, this has the opposite effect. People feel engaged when we focus the conversation on them because it's a way of showing interest. When someone feels that another person is interested in them, they start to feel connected.

Focus more on being *interested* than on being *interesting*.

There are some great books on how to start, continue, and end conversations effectively and comfortably. (I've written several myself, including *How to Communicate with Confidence*.) Most are filled with tips and techniques, so I won't include them here. The best help I can give you is to recognize the two most powerful tools you have available to make your conversations successful: *active listening* and *"go-deeper" questions*.

Active listening

It's amazing that people don't listen more than they do, especially when we know how we feel when someone listens to us. Listening is the quickest way to launch a conversation and move it forward. For one thing, it makes the other person feel comfortable with you because you're showing interest. But also, it's simply a lot easier to listen than to talk for most people:

- You don't have to think of a bunch of stuff to talk about. When you listen deeply without focusing on what you'll say when they finish talking, you'll hear what's important to them. If you pay attention, they're giving you a list of topics they care about.

- Once you've heard their areas of interest or experience, you'll be able to find common ground from your own experience. Since you know what you both care about, you can jump into areas you share in common with confidence that you'll both be interested.
- When you talk about those areas of shared interest, you'll both enjoy the conversation more. That puts your relationship on a fast track for future conversations. You'll be savoring the connection, even though you're at the level of small talk. That becomes the foundation for getting into big talk.

Small talk is where trust grows, and listening shows that you value the person you're talking to. When trust grows, it becomes safer to talk about deeper issues. You've proven that you weren't just waiting for your chance to talk, and you genuinely want to know more and enjoy the other person.

Today, people are starved to have someone listen to them. That's why it's so powerful when it happens, and it's a tool you can use easily with anyone. Active listening sets the stage for taking a conversation to the next level and starting to explore deeper issues. It's not a manipulative technique; it's just a commonsense approach to connecting that's based on caring about the other person. Focus outward instead of inward, and you'll be practicing a world-class communication skill.

"Go-deeper" questions

What if you're talking to someone who's already a good listener, and they're trying to do the same with you? If you're both committed to learning about the other person and putting the focus on them, it's OK. Both people are getting their needs met (the need to be heard and valued).

When that person asks you a question about yourself, it's appropriate to answer that question. Just make sure you don't turn it into an opportunity to tell your life story, which makes the conversation one-sided. Answer their question briefly, preferably with a single response. Then see how they respond. If they ask a follow-up question to go deeper, feel free to answer appropriately.

At the same time, look for opportunities to mirror their question back to them: "So, that's been my experience. What about you—what's your experience in that same area?" A real conversation isn't just one person doing all the asking and the other person doing all the answering. Conversations become engaging when there's give-and-take and both people can participate equally.

It's kind of like playing tennis. One person serves, then the other person returns that serve. That pattern continues until the end of that set, and a new set begins. If one person does all the sharing in a conversation, it would be like one player hitting balls at a person who doesn't have a racket.

The difference is that you're not serving tennis balls; you're serving questions. You're not giving your thoughts on something, hoping the other person is interested. You're asking them for their thoughts, then asking questions to dig deeper and satisfy your growing curiosity. One study said, "People have conversations to accomplish some combination of two major goals: information exchange (learning) and impression management (liking). Recent research shows that asking questions achieves both."[3]

Closed-end questions can be answered with just one word. Usually, they don't move a conversation forward, so we should avoid them. The exception is early in a conversation to get some information points on the table. Asking small-talk questions becomes effective when they're immediately followed with a go-deeper question. Instead of just asking a closed question such as "So, where did you go to school?" follow it up with go-deeper questions such as:

"What was your major?"
"Why did you pick that school?"
"Did you live on campus?"

Then, if the conversation progresses, you can head to the next level of go-deeper questions:

"I've heard that a lot of people end up working in a field that's totally different from their college major. What about you?"
"Did your school meet the expectations you had when you picked it?"
"Since you didn't live on campus, do you feel like you missed out on much of the campus life?"

This process of active listening and asking go-deeper questions doesn't require any preparation. It's amazingly simple, and it will be your greatest resource in any conversation. All you do is:

1. Talk less, ask questions more.
2. Listen to the answers and ask more questions.

I've talked to many people about their initial experiences meeting someone, such as in a social setting. When I asked how it went, here's the most common response I hear: "They didn't ask me enough questions."

Dale Carnegie, in his classic book *How to Win Friends and Influence People*, simply said, "Ask questions the other person will enjoy answering."[4] Talk about what they've brought up and ask questions about it. That shows them you're listening, not just repeating what they said. You're exercising your curiosity to go deeper with something you're interested in.

If you do nothing else but master these two skills, you'll be amazed at how engaging your conversations will become—and how comfortable you'll feel.

Tips for Talking

Consider these suggestions as you hold conversations with people:

Don't rush. Good conversations are like a gourmet meal; they take time to come out well. When you try to rush with people, it takes longer to build a relationship. When you take your time to savor the conversation, complete it, and leave the other person better than you found them, you build the relationship more quickly.

Make it a dialogue, not a monologue. Remember the tennis example; pay attention to the give-and-take, and make sure it goes both ways. If you find yourself talking too much, start asking more questions. Make sure you're asking open-ended questions so they can't give yes or no answers. If one topic isn't working, tell a brief story from your own experience and ask for their thoughts. It's an easy way to move the conversation in a new direction.

Learn something new. Approach every conversation with the goal of learning something new from the other person. Even if you know a person well and talk often, always go on an expedition of discovery.

Stay positive. It's easy to focus on negative perspectives because they're often common ground for people.

Avoid the risk of the energy of the conversation spiraling downward and shift topics as needed.

Be a matchmaker. You end your first conversation with someone at an event, and you've learned new things about that person. Remember those things—and when you have a conversation with someone else, see if there are any similarities. If so, introduce the two of them and note the common ground you discovered. You've saved them the effort of starting from scratch.

Give more than you get. Don't look for what another person can do for you; just build into them instead. Let the relationship grow at a natural pace, simply for the sake of connection. Once that takes place, you might be able to approach them for their help on something. Don't make that your goal; make the relationship your goal. Otherwise, you risk being seen as a high-pressure salesperson looking to close the deal.

Focus 100 percent. In any conversation, make the other person feel like they're the only one in the room. Maintain your focus and eye contact, so they don't feel like you're watching the clock or looking for a better opportunity. End the conversation when you've reached a natural ending point rather than forcing small talk to keep things going. Make a clean, refreshing break.

It's Easier Than You Think

If you struggle with basic conversations, studying the basics of communicating with others will come in handy. At the same time, it's not that hard to get started. The perspectives we've covered in this chapter are enough to begin your journey.

Look at the opportunities you have in the next few weeks. Are you attending a social event that makes you a little nervous?

Will you be in a team meeting or corporate conference that you'd rather avoid? Do you have a one-on-one meeting scheduled with your boss or a coffee date with a challenging colleague? Where will you be encountering people you don't know?

Don't try to make it perfect. Just make it happen. The risks aren't as risky as you think, and the rewards could be more rewarding than you realize. Take the first step to connect, then try out a few of these ideas.

I promise you it'll go better than you expected. Keep doing it, and it'll become more natural than you could imagine.

CHAPTER 9

Plan Your Approach

Customize Your Strategy

Success isn't about how much money you make, it's about the difference you make in people's lives.

Michelle Obama

When I teach a seminar in a hotel conference room, I want to make sure the room is the right temperature. If it gets too warm, people get drowsy and inattentive. If it gets too cold, they can't concentrate. It might not seem as important as the seminar content, but it's critical to get it right or people disengage.

As soon as I arrive, I find the thermostat in the room. Sometimes I can adjust it myself, while other times I need to call a staff person to change it for me. I do this first because of the impact it makes on the event. I want the temperature exactly right before anyone arrives. My goal is that they never notice the temperature because it's "just right."

It didn't take long for me to realize that the thermostats in different rooms aren't all calibrated equally. I discovered that the perfect temperature for most conference rooms is 72.5 degrees Fahrenheit (I bought a small digital thermometer that I'd keep up front where I was presenting). If I set the room thermostat to that temperature, some rooms would be sweltering while others would be frigid. By starting the process early in the day, I had time to learn the proper setting for that particular thermostat before people arrived.

When it comes to reading a room, most people think they can adapt to whatever the "temperature" is. Some rooms feel emotionally cold; some are heated; some are just right. These people accept the temperature but never think about changing it. *This is just the way it is*, they think.

But you're not most people. The fact that you're reading this book tells me you don't just want to read the room; you want to influence the room. Sure, having the ability to read the room will make you feel a lot better in that room. That's a good place to start, but not to stay. You want to make the room a better place for others because you are in it.

In other words, a thermometer informs you of the temperature of the room. It tells you about the present. A thermostat allows you to change the temperature of the room. It helps you influence the future.

Floating Downstream versus Charting a Course

When I was growing up in Phoenix, my friends and I would occasionally take rubber inner tubes down to the Salt River. We'd have someone drive us a few miles upstream and drop us off. Then we'd blow the tubes up and use them to float down the river. We couldn't do much steering because we were lying on top of the tubes, and our arms and legs weren't really in the water. We could lean over the side and splash a bit to nudge ourselves in a new direction, but it wasn't very precise. Mostly, we went where the river took us.

Years later, I went on a whitewater rafting trip on the Green River in Utah. It was exactly the opposite experience because we were sitting in a raft with paddles in our hands. The current was strong, and we weren't floating wherever it took us. Our guides knew the route through the rapids and coached us on exactly how we needed to take control of where we went. If we didn't, the outcome could be tragic.

If there was unusually rough water ahead, we'd paddle to the side of the river, get off the rafts, and hike up a hill to scout the coming rapids. From there, the guides would point out exactly what the current was doing, where the dangers were, and how long it would be before we hit smooth water again. They told us step-by-step what we needed to do to make it through safely. We knew it would be challenging, but those few minutes of preparation gave us the confidence we needed. We'd determined what was ahead and how to manage it instead of just hoping for the best.

Reading a room isn't all that different. It might not seem as life-threatening as whitewater rafting, but the stakes are just as high. We don't want to just survive in the environment we're walking into; we want to thrive.

Most people in any room are floating on inner tubes rather than being intentional about navigating the rapids. They're bobbing along, hoping they don't drown. Others might feel comfortable but aren't thinking about the impact they could make. They're simply using up time and energy by paddling without a sense of direction. As Zig Ziglar often said, "If you aim at nothing, you'll hit it every time."[1]

I've Got Data—Now What?

Everyone reads the room when they enter it, whether they know it or not. Without the process we've been describing, that read is probably not accurate—but they're still taking in information based on what they see.

The problem comes when they make assumptions and believe those assumptions are accurate without digging deeper. They've created a mental map of the details of the event, then take action based on that map. They've already decided the map is accurate and don't question it.

It's like the four-year-old who announces, "I'm six feet tall." When asked how he figured that, he responds, "I measured myself with this ruler I just made."

Earlier, we talked about the value of starting with a hypothesis—an educated guess about what's going on in the room. By now you've spent time observing the room (big picture) and the people in the room (small picture). You've initiated a few connections and had initial conversations. You've decided whether you feel comfortable in the room or not and have a sense of what's really going on.

You're already ahead of most people in the room because you're being intentional. You're not just a participant; you're paying attention. You want to use what you've discovered to feel comfortable and confident in that room, but you also want to make a difference.

So, what's next? It's time to test your hypothesis. Based on what has happened in these initial observations and conversations, does it seem accurate? Or does the data you've collected point to a different outcome? In other words, you read the room initially when you entered. Now that you've done some "research," see if you're reading it differently. Maybe you thought the tone of the room seemed subdued, and people were concerned about what would be discussed. Then you joined a few conversations and realized that people had heard what was going to be announced, and it was good news that put them at ease about a big change they had been anxious about. Yes, the room was subdued, but because they were all breathing a sigh of relief—not because they were afraid of what was coming.

"But wait," you say. "This sounds like I'm supposed to pull away from the group, open my laptop, and analyze my findings on a spreadsheet. Can't I just be present at the event?"

That's not what I'm suggesting. This process is more of a change of mindset than anything else. It enables you to be fully present at any event but also fully aware of your surroundings. It means you're not just floating down the river; you're paying attention to where the current is taking you (and everyone around you) and grabbing a paddle to make sure you have the greatest possible advantage as you read the room.

You won't read the room once and be done. You'll be using the process continuously throughout every situation. You'll still be able to engage in conversations, enjoy your interactions, and make a contribution. You'll just be aware of what you're doing, why you're doing it, and how you're doing it. You'll be attending with intention.

Consider these scenarios:

- You're at a corporate dinner that includes people you know as well as others you don't. Your first instinct is to find a way to sit with the people you know well. At the same time, this is an opportunity to make a few key connections with people who could be valuable for your career. Some might be people with influence, while others just seem interesting and could add to the positive side of your job.

  Do your research ahead of time to find out who will be attending and decide who you'd like to approach. See if any of your friends know that person and would be willing to introduce you. If not, approach them yourself with a quick expression of gratitude for something they've done recently.

Make the conversation about them, and focus on the relationship instead of what they can do for you. Do it right away, then try to make a second, short connection before the event is over.

- Your sales team is visiting a prospective client and meeting with five of their key stakeholders, exploring the chance to work together. You'll be meeting for the whole morning to discuss possibilities.

  During the conversation, listen carefully and find someone on the other team you have some common ground with. When you take your first break, approach that person and bring up the subject: "So, you said you grew up in Texas? So did I. What part? How did you end up here?" Don't talk about the subject of the meeting; just make a human connection. When the meeting continues, you'll have the beginnings of a relationship with one person—which can impact the rest of the discussion.
- You know your coworkers well and know what each person typically brings to your weekly staff meeting. One person always shoots down any new ideas, while another tries to encourage anyone who speaks by flattering them about how amazing their suggestion is (even if it's not). Someone else stays quiet, but you know they'll be sharing their opinion after the meeting.

  Instead of seeing these reactions as "business as usual," think carefully through what each person's paradigm might be that causes them to respond the way they do. With that preparation, create a new alternative you could use with that person that might get a different response.

  When someone is bringing up a new idea, you know that Tom almost always shoots it down right

> away—simply because it's new. Instead of waiting for his critique, jump in quickly: "Before we get too far into this, I'd love to hear Tom's perspective. He sees things that nobody else thinks of, and it might help our conversation to get his ideas."
>
> You could do the same with the quiet person who rarely contributes by dropping by their desk to check in. "Just curious—what did you think of that idea Erin brought up? I know you've had similar situations, and I immediately wondered about your perspective."

That's being proactive. Even if they've been paying attention, most people simply react to what they see and go with the flow, hoping things will go well. They're not in the river with a purpose, making choices about where they go. They simply float along with the current.

If you want to achieve different results from everyone else, you want to make different choices than everyone else. As Earl Nightingale said, "If you don't have a good model for success, just look at what everyone else is doing and do the opposite."[2]

Always Aware

A few years ago, I was teaching a seminar in a large midwestern city. The city police chief was in the class and invited me to have lunch with him after the morning session. He seemed like a down-to-earth guy with a great sense of humor, so I was looking forward to connecting.

I got to the restaurant before he did and found a table up against a window. I took the window seat facing the restaurant interior, leaving the other seat open facing the window.

When he walked up, his first words were, "Get up. You're in my seat." He said it in a joking way, but I sensed he meant it. When I didn't move right away, he said, "No, I'm serious. I need to sit there."

He couldn't have been more warm and friendly as we talked, and we had a great conversation. When it was just about time to leave, I asked him about his choice of seats. "You're off duty today, right?"

"Yep."

"So, why did you need to sit in that seat? Do you need to see what's going on even if you're not on duty?"

He replied, "It's my training. And my experience. Even while I'm having a great conversation, I'm completely aware of everything that's happening around the room. I'm reading the room constantly. It's almost subconscious now, even while I'm 100 percent engaged when I'm with somebody. But I know what to look for, and I never shut that off. Nobody else is doing that—just me. If anything is a little off, I'm ready to take action if I need to.

"That's why I always take a seat where I can see everything and where there's nobody behind me," he finished. "And if anything were to happen, you'd be glad you gave me that seat."

That was a perfect example of why we learn to read a room. We probably won't be fighting crime, but we have a whole different perspective when we're conditioned to know what's going on around us. Over time it will become subconscious—almost second nature. We can be completely engaged in what's going on around us and completely enjoy our encounters. But everything will be in the context of the bigger picture, and we'll be able to make decisions about what to do next because of what we observe.

Your Customized Strategy

Your way of reading a room will be just that—your way. You'll create it and hone it over time because it exactly fits your skills, gifts, and temperament. If you're an introvert, you don't have to pretend you're outgoing. If you're an extrovert, you can be your gregarious self with intention. Whatever your approach, you'll be responding and not reacting.

Let's say you'll be attending a corporate team meeting in a few minutes, so you start practicing your new skill of exploring. The agenda says you'll be discussing a recent policy change that's controversial. You know it could be volatile, so you observe the tone of the room and the people in the room: who's talking with who, who looks energized, who looks distracted or bored. You also see there's a pile of handouts on the front table, so you assume they'll be passed out for discussion.

Based on that, you create a quick hypothesis: "Due to the topic and the expressions I see in this room, there's a good chance people are going to get upset. I know how each of these people usually responds, so there's probably going to be conflict. Two people will be upset and vocal, two will be passive-aggressive and snarky, three others won't talk but will have thoughts that we really need to hear, three will be positive, and two others won't care."

Now you're ready to test your hypothesis by entering the conversation. You'll still be observing, but it'll be in the context of your hypothesis. You might discover quickly that it was correct, or you might see it move in a whole different direction. Your careful exploration initially will be the filter you use to interpret what you see, and that becomes your guide for deciding what action to take. Having the mindset of observing what's happening (like the police chief) enables you to determine the significance of what you see.

The meeting begins, and you begin watching for those different perspectives as well as noticing who's participating and who's not—especially the latter. Most people just hear the input from those who are contributing, but you're also watching the facial expressions and body language of those who are doing more listening than talking.

One of your colleagues made a few statements to express her concerns but quit sharing after her comments were overlooked. You know her input is usually valuable and well-thought-out, and it seems like her ideas could keep the group from making some costly decisions. What should you do?

Most people didn't notice the things you noticed, so you have the opportunity to explore even deeper. You're not sure if she felt overlooked and upset or if it just looked like it. You don't need to mention to the group that they were ignoring her, which she might find embarrassing. Just shine a light on her briefly in a way that gives her the opportunity to share her thoughts—if she wants to.

"Can I jump in here for a second and revisit something?" you could say. "When we were talking about the impact of the new change, Sharon brought up a couple of ideas that sounded valuable, and I just wanted to make sure we didn't miss them. Sharon, do you want to expand on those thoughts so we can make sure—or are you OK with where we're headed?"

You've positioned Sharon to insert her ideas but also to clarify if she's good with the current discussion as is. By being aware of what you observed and making a simple statement, you showed respect for your colleague as well as made sure that valuable information wasn't overlooked by the group.

Over time, you'll gain a reputation as a person who consistently keeps discussions on track. You'll make sure everyone has a chance to contribute if they want to as well as keep the more vocal group members from dominating the discussion.

If you become skilled at exploring, engaging, and envisioning, you'll have the confidence to keep your finger on the pulse of group dynamics. Being your unique self, you'll be able to gently tweak those dynamics so everyone is able to use their unique voice in their unique way.

Eyes Open

That's why it's so important to turn your observations and conversations into a strategy for not just reading the room but working the room. You don't have to be the leader to make a difference. You can use your mindset of paying attention to make things better—to serve the room, which we'll talk about more toward the end of this book.

One example: I was teaching a university class one semester and noticed two students with rather unusual behavior whenever I gave a written test. They sat on opposite sides of the room. After they wrote responses to a few questions, they would set their pencils down and slowly move their fingers as though they were stretching them. I figured their hands were just getting tired from writing (since most students usually write on digital devices instead of paper). I noticed but assumed it was harmless.

After one exam, another student approached me after the class. "I've been noticing something going on in the class, and I'm not sure you see it," she said. "You know those two girls who are always stretching their fingers? They're cheating."

"How do you know?" I asked.

"Because my brother is deaf, and I know sign language. They know it, too—and they're sharing answers across the room. They're signing slowly, but they're cheating."

She wasn't just reading the room; she wanted to impact it. All she did was let me know what she had discovered, and I could take steps to make the process fairer for everyone in the room.

Another example: the education department of a nearby county had a lot of students living in challenging situations (something that happens in school districts across the country). That led to a lot of behavior problems in class as they acted out what was happening in their lives. Without realizing the background, teachers were repeatedly sending misbehaving students to the principal's office.

Finally, someone took the initiative to make a difference. They collaborated on a system where first responders (police, fire, or emergency medical personnel) could use an app to notify a school if a student had been exposed to violence or another traumatic situation. The school would then receive a "Handle with Care" notification, indicating that the child had gone through a challenging event (no specifics given). This permitted the school to make appropriate staff aware of the incident so they could monitor the child and treat them with proportionate sensitivity. Without providing confidential details, it allowed the school to factor that information into behavior issues such as being distracted or sleeping in class, then choose what to do based on that knowledge.

Learn to read a room well, then develop a strategy for your unique contribution to every room you enter. By tapping into your own uniqueness, you'll make a difference that only you can as you "work the room." What does that look like? It's called *execution*—putting your strategy into action to make sure something happens. Let's jump into the next chapter to get results that matter!

CHAPTER 10

Execute Your Strategy

Work the Room

No greater gift there is, than a generous heart.

Yoda

If you've ever taught a teenager to drive, you know you have a lot of emotions around the process. On one hand, you want them to learn the freedom and convenience that comes with having a license. On the other hand, you know—from personal experience—how much is at stake and how much could go wrong. Even if they become the best driver in the world, everybody else is unpredictable. Other people aren't nearly as committed to your teen's safety as you are.

When I was teaching my daughter, Sara, to drive, I wanted her to believe that I knew what I was talking about. I needed her to trust my experience so she would become a good driver. I wanted her to learn from my mistakes instead of having to make her own.

That fell apart the first day we were driving my little Volkswagen Bug in slow, tight circles at the end of a cul-de-sac. A pigeon flew down and landed right in front of the car. Sara stopped because she couldn't see it and didn't want to hit it.

"Go ahead," I said. "We're going so slow that it'll move out of the way if we get too close." Seconds later, we felt the *thump* and saw feathers flying everywhere.

That was the end of my credibility.

She did learn, and years later, I'm completely comfortable when she's behind the steering wheel.

Driving is a lot like reading a room. You can practice the techniques and be proficient at making connections. At the same time, you don't always know what other people are going to do. Their choices might be on a collision course with yours, so you have to be ready for anything.

How do you do that? Practice. A teen can't become a driver who can handle challenging situations by just watching videos about driving. Likewise, we can't handle the challenges of interacting with others by just reading a book about it. We have to *spend time in* the room so we can *read* the room so we can *work* the room.

How to Work a Room without Feeling Like a Politician

I'm using "work the room" cautiously because that phrase has negative overtones usually associated with politicians trying to drum up votes. One dictionary describes it this way: "To 'work the room' is to move through a crowd, greeting people and engaging them in conversation. [It] typically involves a lot of handshaking, hugging, or backslapping as well as plenty of visible enthusiasm."[1]

Just typing that description has me reaching for an antacid. It has the scent of sliminess, of pretending to like people in order to get something from them. It's even tougher for me as an introvert because it sounds like I have to become artificially outgoing if I want to be successful.

We're going to change the definition. Let's move away from sleaziness to sincerity, from fake to genuine, from getting to giving. Let's shift from survival to impact. It will involve the basic skills we've been talking about, practicing them in a way that's absolutely in line with who we are.

This is called *integrity*—where who we are on the outside comes out of who we are on the inside. When we're able to do that, working the room becomes a tool to help us connect with confidence and impact in any situation, no matter what our personality or temperament. We will discuss the specific tips and techniques to use (keep reading), but they'll all be in line with who we really are.

Here's our new definition of working the room: *mastering the skills of connection and conversation with the goal of improving every situation we encounter.*

Navigating Differences

At the same time, working the room will only be effective when we recognize the different temperaments of the other people in the room. I need to be a proficient, experienced driver on the highway, but I also need to be aware of the different "driving styles" of other people. Being a good driver gives me confidence and freedom. Being aware of what other drivers are doing keeps me alive.

The first part of the process for reading a room entails becoming skillful at it (over time, with practice). The second part is to use that skill when interacting with others, navigating the dynamics that come when there are differences. Let's look at a few ways this might play out.

For example, some people function best early in the morning, which is when they have their highest energy and think the most clearly. Other people can barely form coherent words or thoughts for the first few hours of the day but communicate with complete clarity in the evening. If you watch someone long enough, it's not hard to tell which is which. If I'm a morning person and my boss is a night person, I'll schedule a meeting to discuss my career with him at his best time, not mine. I won't make it too late because I'll be at a disadvantage. But I'll avoid a breakfast meeting if I need his full attention.

Or consider remote workers, who often feel left out because they're not in the office to experience the "water cooler" talk and other casual conversations during the day. If I'm the one in the office, I can make sure I send a quick email to a remote colleague whenever something interesting or meaningful comes up so they don't miss out. Quick little gestures like this let people know they are seen.

There might also be differences in the audience. When I'm making a presentation to a group of scientists or engineers, for example, I've learned the importance of emphasizing facts and figures and data. But if I'm speaking to a team of salespeople, I'll focus on actionable techniques for growth. For senior executives, I'll reinforce their desire to make an impact.

And finally, the difference may lie in *you*. The way you see a room might make total sense to you, but another person could have an equally valid but totally different perspective. Recognizing that reality lets you make more powerful connections because you're tapping into the reality of who both of you are—without trying to change each other.

Yes, you can work the room—but only by being real. You're not seeking support or attention; you're focused on positively impacting the experience of others. Do that, and you'll get a lot of support and attention anyway.

A New Approach—Your Approach

I've learned that most things in life can be simpler than I make them. That doesn't feel natural, though. I tend to think if something's going to have great value, the process needs to be big and complicated and well researched and full of big words. If I keep things too simple, I'm afraid people will think it's too pedestrian and move on to something deeper with more pages. I want to be seen as deep, so I use words like *pedestrian* instead of *common* or *ordinary*.

At the same time, I realize the things that have had the greatest impact on me have been simple. Sure, it's good to work through something challenging now and then and figure it out. But I'm affected most when I see something I can apply immediately because it just makes sense.

As I mentioned earlier, I read a bunch of books on the topic of reading and working a room in preparation for writing this book. There were amazing ones and others that seemed more pedestrian (sorry, I had to do that). Almost all of them prescribed a "sure-fire process" that guaranteed success. It felt like the author said, "Here's how I've learned to do it, and it works. If you do it the same way, it'll work for you too."

That's where most of them broke down for me. Anytime we see a "do it this way" prescription, it's almost guaranteed we won't get the same outcomes. Why? Because everyone is unique. We can adapt ideas from such plans but need guidance to customize an approach that exactly fits who we are. It's like those weight loss commercials that show amazing transformation photos but have tiny print at the bottom of the screen that reads, "Weight loss testimonials are in no way a guarantee of results," and "No individual result should be seen as typical."

One author said that we needed to exchange our inner dialogue from *I'm dreading this event* to *I'm going to have fun at this event*. I agree 100 percent, and I also believe it's possible for anyone. But the context was that "fun" was an extroverted party type of environment. For the 30–50 percent of the population who are on the quiet side, that feels like an eternity of hearing fingernails on a chalkboard.

Anyone can have "fun" if they find an environment where they get to be totally themselves. It's when they can enjoy working the room within their own temperament, free from the expectations of others to do it in a certain way. When the skills have been mastered and the approach comes with a sense of confidence, anyone can look forward to working the room with an expectation of success.

Sammy Davis Jr. summarized the idea in his classic song, "I've Gotta Be Me." It's a simple title but packed with truth.

How to Work the Room: The Basics

So, what are the most important things to consider when you're ready to jump in and work the room? Here are some ingredients you can easily adapt to your own style and personality. They're not a guaranteed approach but rather reflect commonsense things that humans respond to.

Smile. I mentioned this one earlier, but when we're nervous, we usually don't know how other people see us. The simplest way to show that you're open for conversation is to smile whenever you make eye contact with another person. It's a universal connecting point. Don't be like the person avoiding eye contact on a bus so no one will choose the seat next to them.

Pay attention. When you're talking to someone, give them direct eye contact to show you're listening. Ask deeper questions to explore what they said. Don't glance at the door or over their shoulder. If you're ready to end the conversation, wrap it up graciously while still being completely attentive, then move on.

Encourage honesty. Avoid flattery like a pandemic. Share encouragement and things you admire and respect about them, but only if it's completely honest. People sense flattery, and it builds a barrier between you.

Assume that others want to connect at a large event. If they didn't, they wouldn't be there. It's not risky; the worst thing that can happen is that they don't engage, and you can move on. The best thing that can happen is that you'll make a new friend.

Talk about them. Make them comfortable by focusing on what they're saying instead of one-upping them with your own story. If they ask, respond. But in general, focus on them. They'll remember you for it.

Say thanks. If there's a genuine reason for gratitude, don't just feel it—express it. Your casual, honest affirmation can make someone's entire week because they probably didn't know their words or actions had impact. Be the person who makes a difference.

Be generous. If there's a resource you can provide or someone you can introduce them to, do it. If you connect them with things and people they can benefit from, you've gone up in value with them.

Focus on names. When you hear someone's name, repeat it. If it's a name that's tough for you to pronounce, ask them for help. Names are important to people, and they'll appreciate the effort to get them right. When meeting someone you haven't seen for a long time, don't assume they remember your name; reintroduce yourself.

Follow up. If you make a positive connection with someone and want to stay in touch, send an invitation via LinkedIn or another appropriate site as soon as possible after the event. Don't accept their invitation to lunch or coffee under pressure if you know it's not going to happen. Just say, "I don't want to say yes now and not be able to make it happen. Let's stay in touch on LinkedIn and go from there."

Plan on learning something new. Each person you connect with has a unique experience and background. If you're meeting them for the first time, it will all be new. If they are a colleague you work with every day, don't assume you know everything about them. Make it your goal to dig deeper and glean something you don't know. You'll be enriched by it, and they'll respect you for drawing it out.

Approach non-celebrities. It's tempting to try to connect with the key players in a room, but the most meaningful connections often come from those who others aren't approaching. They might be quieter on the outside but noisy on the inside—filled with rich experiences and ideas that haven't been tapped.

Stay positive. Your attitude will set the tone for the conversation. Don't get sucked into negative talk; divert them into a focus on the positive, optimistic side. You have the ability to influence the way people feel with your approach.

Bottom line: all of these ideas are ingredients to draw from as you create a recipe for social success. Try them out and decide which ones will become part of your standard approach in every social situation, meeting, or conference setting—anyplace people gather. Once you've crafted a unique way of navigating new situations, you'll be energized by every opportunity.

There's More than Just Reading the Room

In these chapters, we've learned a simple process that's easily customizable, one that will fit you perfectly when you make it your own. That could be the main reason you picked up this book—to learn how to thrive in social situations.

"But wait . . . there's more!" the late-night commercials advertise. Now that you've learned to be comfortable and confident in the room, you'll feel a lot better. But this also gives you an opportunity to make a difference in that room by leading it in new directions. You might be the person at the top with the leadership position, or you might be using "unofficial leadership" through quiet influence. Either way, this is your chance to change the direction of the room—and it's just as simple as the steps we've covered so far. You'll find the strategy in the next section—and it could give you a whole new sense of purpose!

How to Lead a Room (for Influence)

Becoming a leader is kind of like having your first baby:

- There's usually some excitement before it happens, and pain in the process.
- The role doesn't come with instructions.
- The stakes are high because you're going to be responsible for a human being.
- Over time, it can become very rewarding (or very discouraging).
- You're in for the long game.

If you picked up this book because you wanted to feel more confident in the room, you might be tempted to stop here. You've got a handle on the basics now.

Don't quit now—this next section is *exactly* for you! You might be saying, "But I don't want to be a leader." I understand—and it makes sense if we think of the common definition of *leader*: the person at the top who has a ton of responsibility and has to get people to do things. Leaders cast a vision and run the show and have to have the right education and people skills.

Think about what first responders do in a crisis situation. The value they bring doesn't come from their personality or temperament. They're just ordinary people who have been trained to know how to "read the room" when they arrive on the scene and discern exactly what's going on. They don't stop there, though. They have one objective in mind: *to make a difference*.

Imagine a firefighter who goes through training to know how to create order out of chaos and shows up on the scene—but doesn't do anything. They know what needs to be done, and they're confident in their knowledge of how to make the whole situation better. They just don't take action.

"Don't just stand there," we would scream. "Do something!"

Fortunately, that's almost never the case. First responders choose to go into that line of work because they want to make a difference for people. The training isn't just so they'll feel better; it's so they can change things in any situation.

That's why this book is different. We *need* to know how to read the rooms we enter, both for gaining confidence and feeling comfortable. That's easy when we know the basics and practice them.

But there's a deeper reason for getting to that point: *the ability to make a difference*. When you read a room well, you can make things better in that room. It might be your influence with one person or with an entire group. Your confident presence naturally leads to *impact*.

In this section, we'll start with a fresh definition of leadership, a customized, personal one that emerges from who you are and lets you craft your own description of what it will involve. You might have the formal title of leader, or you might be just one more person in the room. Either way, you will learn what it takes to lead a room to make a difference.

Let's jump in!

CHAPTER 11

Leading the Room

> If you want to make everyone happy, don't be a leader. Sell ice cream.
>
> Unknown

Years ago, I saw a cartoon in the local paper showing hundreds of lemmings running toward the edge of a cliff. (There's a common apocryphal belief that these small rodents have a habit of following each other, even to their death.) The cartoon shows the lemming at the front teetering on the edge in front of the surging crowd, yelling, "I don't want to be the leader anymore!"

Some people seem to have been created for the challenges of leadership. They're outgoing and energetic, and people gravitate to them. They're capable of making important decisions under pressure, crafting policy, and getting others to follow along willingly.

Other people respect those leaders because they're good at what they do. At the same time, they have no desire to be in that position. Why? Because that description is the opposite of how they're wired. They want to make a difference, but not in that way. They might be more reflective or cautious, and they do their best work in smaller, quieter settings—maybe even with just one person. So being a leader isn't on their radar.

On the surface, it makes sense that not everyone can (or should) be that kind of leader. We've accepted that description of leadership as "the way it's done." Unfortunately, here's how the thought process plays out in our minds:

Thought #1: *A leader is an outgoing visionary who exudes confidence and gets people to move in a direction.*

Thought #2: *I'm not outgoing, I'm not a visionary, and I don't exude confidence—and nobody is following me.*

Thought #3: *That means I can't be a leader (so I'm not interested).*

We each have two choices. One choice would be to continue to think leadership isn't for us.

The other choice is one that could change our lives. It goes down a path less traveled—one that redefines what it means to be a leader. It changes the common definition to one that not only fits who we are but motivates us to move ahead with purpose.

So, first, we need a new definition.

Becoming a Fresh Kind of Leader

Amelia is a self-proclaimed introvert with no desire to be "at the top." That role is way out of her comfort zone and holds no attraction for her. For a variety of reasons, she often finds herself at company events or social gatherings where clinking glasses and overlapping conversations are the background music in the room. She's never been naturally confident in these situations but studied the basics of how to read what is happening around her and navigate those events well.

Instead of being the center of attention, she discovered a great response whenever she approached the quietest people in the room. They responded well to her initiative with fascinating conversation because she "went first" and wanted to listen. She also became skilled at helping others overcome those awkward moments and deftly connecting them with each other. They made new connections and found common ground, and nobody had to force business cards on each other; they asked for them.

Amelia began to look forward to those events because she could tell she was making a difference for a number of people by creating an environment where they felt valued and connected. Soon that became her reputation, and people looked forward to her presence. They saw her as their leader because she knew how to make their lives better.

This type of leadership is available to anyone.

Where do we begin? By putting aside our preconceived notions. Even as we learn new things, we often hang on to our old paradigms, practices, biases, and preconceptions. We assume they're still applicable, but what if they're getting in the way of moving in new directions? It's time to be willing to let go of the familiar so we can lead in new, relevant ways.

There is a place for the traditional leader. If that's you, this is the chance to refine your skills to make the greatest possible impact. You feel like you're made for this, and you're right.

At the same time, there's also a place for the kind of unofficial leadership that's available to everyone. If you've never considered the possibility of being a change-maker because of your temperament, this is your chance to capitalize on that temperament to make a difference you never imagined was possible. By being completely yourself, you can gain a sense of purpose and mission in every situation and impact the lives of everyone you meet.

It's time to move from being an observer to being a catalyst for change!

Setting the Angel Free

I don't write books. Even though this is my tenth book, I don't create the polished work of art that we call a book. I write manuscripts.

When I submit my best effort to the publisher, those manuscripts have a lot of really good ideas and engaging stories that are kind of jumbled together and wander off on rabbit trails, mixed with paragraphs that need to be in a different order. If you read my manuscripts, you might find a few good ideas—but they wouldn't be obvious. Discovering the best thoughts in there is often like finding rainbows in a mud puddle.

Fortunately, I have an editor who makes each of my manuscripts worth reading. She sees the potential the way a mother of a teenager knows there's a good kid inside trying to find their way out. She doesn't add anything except suggestions; she shapes and hones and trims away all the stuff that doesn't work and shouldn't be there. She also has the courage to cut out my favorite stories that are fun to tell but do nothing to reinforce the message. Then she polishes it so it looks like a new car on the showroom floor.

I write the manuscript. She handcrafts it into a book.

It's similar to the apocryphal way Michelangelo described the process of turning a block of stone into a finished sculpture: "I saw the angel in the marble and carved until I set him free."[1]

So, let's cut away the old definitions of leadership that may hold us back. We need to release ideas that are familiar to adopt ones that turn us in a new, powerful direction.

Writing a New Description

Have you ever worked for an ineffective leader? You think, *How in the world did they ever get put into that position?* Most of the time, they've moved into a leadership position because someone was needed and they were the easiest choice. They often don't get any training in how to lead but feel like they can never admit they don't know what they're doing, so they never get the help they need. They pretend to be confident and become more forceful because they don't know what else to do. It's a cover for their feelings of incompetence, which they don't feel free to admit.

Here are some of the characteristics of ineffective leadership:

- *Dominant*. Tells people what to do instead of helping them make their own unique contribution.
- *Self-centered*. Focuses on their own needs and desires at the expense of what others want and need.
- *Micromanaging*. Controls every detail of what others do.
- *Intolerant of mistakes*. Punishes errors, which keeps people from growing, risking, and trying.
- *Not seeking or valuing feedback*. Has all the answers and doesn't listen to input from others.
- *Clueless*. Doesn't recognize their shortcomings, so they don't try to get help and fix them.
- *Focused on short-term results*. Is more concerned about looking good in the present than making the best choices for the future.

If that's how we've experienced leadership, is it any wonder we don't want to go there?

So, what are the characteristics of effective leadership?

- *Inspires.* Motivates others by inviting them into a story and helping them see why it's important.
- *Guides.* Shows people both the path and the pitfalls so they can travel together on the journey.
- *Empowers.* Guides people without micromanaging by building trust with them.
- *Accountable.* Takes personal responsibility for their own actions and choices, which shows others how it can be done.
- *Communicates.* Listens and empathizes, valuing the contributions of others and creating a structure that makes it safe for others to communicate.

A leader works to bring out the best in others, not just tell them what to do. It's about getting others to do their best because they feel part of something important. As author Brené Brown says, "A leader is anyone who takes responsibility for finding the potential in people and processes and has the courage to develop that potential."[2]

Did you notice the word *anyone*? Yes, that definition does apply to people who have the title and position of a leader. But here's the best news: *the same description fits "unofficial leaders" who inspire everyone they meet to get better.*

That's all of us. When you enter any room, you can be a leader immediately. It might be with just one person or the whole group. You'll be confident, and you're ready to make a difference. It's not about you anymore; it's about making people better when they leave than when they came in.

The Dictionary Says . . .

When I started researching this chapter, I assumed I needed to find a common definition of leadership, then create a better version. Eventually, I decided against coming up with my own. Instead, I looked for a definition that was simple enough to remember but powerful enough to fit well into our discussion of leading and reading a room. It needed to be something anyone could easily put into practice to make an impact, no matter what their temperament.

I finally landed on one from John Maxwell, one of the most prolific voices on leadership today. He's written dozens of books that provide practical resources and perspective for people who want to lead others and is known for writing content that's so profound it almost seems simplistic—which is why it works.

Here's his practical definition, which we'll be using throughout our discussion: *leadership is influence, nothing more, nothing less.*[3]

That's good news for everyone; we all have the ability to influence others. *Influence* means that when you're in the presence of another person, your words, actions, and attitude show up on their radar (assuming they're paying attention, which is another issue for later). When they notice, they have a reaction and often think differently as a result.

This goes beyond the skills of leadership we usually associate with formal leaders. It adds another dimension that allows everyone to lead others through the influence they can have in each person's life.

Some leaders (usually ones with the title) get people to do things through *extrinsic* motivation. If people perform, they get paid. If they do their job well, they get promoted. These leaders primarily motivate people by giving them something in return for performance. If they stop giving those things, the person isn't motivated and stops performing.

Other leaders (often the "unofficial" leaders) use *intrinsic* motivation, drawing from what's inside each person. Those people choose to contribute because they want to, not because they're forced. They're internally motivated and excited about a shared vision of what things could be like. These leaders don't primarily motivate people by giving them things but by inspiring them.

The first approach uses *direction*. The second approach uses *influence*.

That's why the second approach works so well whenever you enter a room of any type. If you walked into a party and started directing people and telling them what to do, you'd get a pretty cold response. But when your goal is to influence, you simply relate to people with the goal of inspiring them to become better than they are in that moment.

Knowing the basic skills needed to enter a room and knowing that we have the ability to make the room better through our unique influence, we can actually look forward to entering a room whenever we have the opportunity. We've moved from being uncomfortable to comfortable, from cautious to confident.

As we do this, we develop confidence that we can lead a room in our own unique way.

Simple Influence

Influence is intentional. We're not primarily focused on our own agenda, like a stereotypical high-pressure salesperson trying to convince people to buy something they don't really want. It means we enter each room with a mission that's uniquely our own: to discover what matters to another person and help them move closer to satisfying that desire.

Influence leadership isn't about getting things done through other people (though that's often a byproduct). It's about enabling personal development and self-discovery. An influential leader helps others discover strengths they didn't know they had (or kickstart the ones that have gone dormant over time). They also help them use those strengths to handle challenges they face, then to grow as a result. The outcome for the other person? Organizational success as well as personal growth and satisfaction.

You don't have to stand up front to be a leader. Your ability to choose the right people to influence could impact the entire group from behind the scenes. Instead of being the up-front personality who leads everyone, you can make a genuine, empathic connection with each person you meet. You'll influence them by impacting them individually. That impact ripples out as they also impact the people in their sphere of influence. By influencing individuals, you influence the people they're connected to as well.

That's genuine leadership—influencing each person so they'll be contagious to others.

It Starts with You

Leadership isn't a position; it's an extension of who you are. Leadership begins with your reputation and credibility. The more people trust you, the more they'll listen to your words and the more influence you'll have. You can't demand influence; you earn it over time.

We've all been impressed by people who seemed confident and dynamic and chose to follow them. But over time, we started to see the inconsistencies in their character or their approach and realized they weren't trustworthy. Their influence on us weakened because we'd seen through the facade. At the same time, we've also known people who weren't as charismatic but built trust over time. They were consistent in their approach, demonstrating trustworthiness in each situation. The more we were around them, the more we trusted their character and competence.

When that happened, they had more influence on us. In other words, they became a leader we could trust.

Where does your journey to being a trusted influencer begin? By becoming a person of character. When you work on who you are on the inside, it leaks out on the outside. People might not say anything, but they will sense it. They'll be drawn to your consistency as you demonstrate your commitment and authenticity.

Sure, it's important to learn traditional leadership skills as your influence grows. But the place to start is with character. Focusing on the skills without the inner character is like painting a house that's riddled with termites. It may look fresh and bright on the outside, but it will eventually crumble when the storms hit.

As you start influencing those around you, don't focus on your leadership abilities. Focus on becoming a caring catalyst who develops leadership in others. As you influence them, they'll unconsciously begin to do the same with others. Encourage others in this way, and their leadership skills will grow from the inside out.

Don't make it your goal to have people look at you and say, "They are the leader." Make it your goal to help them see themselves as leaders. Guide them into discovering their own strengths and character traits, then encourage them to use that foundation for influencing others.

CHAPTER 12

Leading by Influence in a Virtual Room

If we have data, let's look at data. If all we have are opinions, let's go with mine.

Unknown

"Death by Zoom." That caption was coined in 2020, a few months into the pandemic. It reflected the new normal that had become a part of most employees' worlds.

Before the pandemic shut everything down, most people got up and went to work each day. If someone did work from home, they were probably a "creative" such as an artist or writer or another self-employed person. They were the exception, and their daily commute was usually from one side of the house to the other. Millions of jealous commuters were thinking, *I wish I could work from home too*.

Well, they got their wish. The problem was that nobody knew how to do it, and it was messy. Companies scrambled to figure out how to keep operating without having people physically in the same room, and those people had to figure out what working from home looked like. In an environment where they usually went to relax after a full day of effort, they now had to navigate the dynamics of doing everything in the same space.

Virtual video meetings had existed before that, but they weren't part of many employees' daily reality. Occasionally, someone would make a Skype call to connect with someone in another state or country, but most things happened in person. If you wanted to talk to a colleague, you'd walk down the hall. If you wanted to meet with a distant client, you'd hop on a plane.

Without warning, video calls became the only viable option. People who were comfortable in their daily routines had to start from scratch. Not only did they have to learn a new technology just to survive but they also had to learn new ways of relating to each other. The old "rules" didn't seem to fit anymore. Did the dress code change because they were working from home? How did bosses know if their employees were actually working? How could people stay focused and avoid the distractions of the television, the refrigerator, and naps?

One of my clients was a large bank in Los Angeles. I met with one man on a regular basis in his office, and he was always dressed impeccably in a suit and tie. The first time he showed up onscreen when he had to work from home, he was sitting on the edge of his bed in a tattered T-shirt and shorts, with uncombed hair, looking like he had just crawled out of bed. It caught me off guard at first, until I realized that everyone was trying to figure this new thing out.

No matter how good someone was at reading the room, it didn't translate well to a virtual environment:

- You didn't have the advantage of simply being physically present in the same room with each other.

- You could see other people's faces onscreen, but hardly anyone used normal gestures. If they did, you couldn't see them because they were out of the frame.
- You didn't know how to effectively speak up to comment on something, so people ended up talking over each other.
- You could see someone's eyes, but there was no eye contact. Since they were looking at their screen instead of their camera, it seemed like they were looking slightly off-camera.
- If you raised your eyebrows when making a comment, no one changed their facial expressions in response like they would in person.
- People didn't feel comfortable on camera and would often turn their camera off—so you had no idea what they were doing or how they were responding.
- People weren't accustomed to the mute button and would forget to unmute when they were speaking—so nobody heard them. Or forget to mute themselves entirely and fail to realize people could hear everything going on around them.

No one realized how exhausting it would be to communicate in that setting for hours at a time. When we can't read a room the way we're used to, it's tough to know how to lead that room with our influence.

Now, a few years later, we've gotten used to virtual video connecting—but that doesn't mean we know how to thrive in that environment. Fortunately, it's possible for anyone to master the skills of reading a virtual room. A few basic considerations can make a world of difference, both in your confidence and in the influence you can have in any room (whether you're the formal leader or not).

When You're a Participant

Most in-person meetings have someone who's running the show. The rest are participants with different levels of involvement. There are always a few who speak early and often, responding to comments and questions and presenting their ideas. Others will speak up occasionally but mostly just listen. The rest of the group doesn't contribute unless they're called on. This doesn't necessarily mean they're not engaged; they might just be on the quieter side, listening more and processing before talking.

In a physical room, it's not difficult to read if we use the four steps we talked about earlier: Observe the Setting, Engage with People, Plan Your Approach, and Execute Your Strategy. We have the advantage of being in the same place, seeing everything going on around us, and hearing all parts of the discussion. That's true in any context, even a social setting where we're observing people, listening to them, and getting a sense of what's happening. We can easily approach anyone and start a conversation to build a connection and explore their thoughts.

It's different in a virtual room. Unless you're one of the extroverts in the room, it's challenging to be seen and heard. That feels like it might limit your ability to influence the room because you're in the shadows. You know you need to be as visible as if you were in a physical space—but how?

In a virtual setting, everything changes. The rules have shifted, and you need different strategies if you're going to stay visible enough to make a difference. Fortunately, there are simple changes you can make, no matter what anyone else does—and you don't have to become the life of the party to make them work:

- If an agenda hasn't been provided ahead of the call, ask your meeting contact if it's available. Agendas often are not distributed because nobody reads them. If you can get a copy, read it so you can gather your thoughts and data and be ready to contribute.

- Enter the virtual room early. If you're one of the first ones on the call, you can greet people as they join, and they'll recognize your presence. As others sign in, they'll naturally look to see who's already there—which will include you. If you come in late, nobody notices—and probably won't as the meeting progresses.
- Make sure your lighting is good and the camera shows you clearly. In fact, look around on your next call and notice how many people are in the dark or hard to see clearly. It's worth the effort to make sure you stand out in the group.
- Put your laptop (or separate camera) on a few books or a stand so the camera is slightly higher than eye level. Not only will that make it look more natural for conversation, it will improve your posture (which is the only body language people will see).
- When you contribute, use simple gestures that can be seen easily on the screen such as thumbs-up and OK signs. Glance at yourself as you talk to make sure your gestures come across well.
- Let your face show engagement, just like you would in an in-person meeting. Most people are expressionless on virtual calls, so you'll stand out. At the least, smile when it's appropriate.
- Keep your camera on as much as you can, but turn it off occasionally during a longer meeting. It's tough having people looking at you for an extended time, and you'll stay fresher with breaks. Going off-camera also allows you to stand and move a bit.
- Avoid the temptation to multitask. Everyone does it sometimes, but staying engaged helps you have more

influence because you'll have more focus, more to contribute, and more creativity to follow up with ideas after the meeting. Plus, people might not know you're checking your email or playing solitaire but they'll see the glazed-over look in your eyes. If you look disengaged, you aren't in a position to make a difference.

- When you want to make a comment, don't wait for a chance to squeeze it in like everyone else does (and risk having people talk over you). Simply raise your hand and keep it up until someone acknowledges it. Someone will usually notice, and you'll set a tone for others to do the same thing. You could also suggest it to the meeting leader as a best practice for the team. It's a simple way you can influence the conversational flow by example.
- Master your mute button. Stay muted when you're not talking but make sure you're ready to unmute as soon as you're asked a question.
- Be concise when you speak. Make your point, back it up briefly with reasons or data, then stop. Get a reputation for not wasting people's time by talking in circles.

If you're going to read the room and influence the room, people have to know you're in the room (whether virtual or in person). That's why the first step is to make sure that happens.

When You're in Charge

If you're the one leading the call, it's your job to make sure you set the tone and strategy for getting maximum benefit for the participants. There are simple things you can do to make those calls something people look forward to because they're a good use of their time. Here are some of the key areas of awareness.

Presenting

It's easy to lose your energy when presenting to a video room because there's not as much energy coming from participants. You can't pick up on their gestures or facial expressions because it looks like they're disengaged. If you let that pull you down, it will be contagious. Just because people aren't nodding, don't assume they're not engaged. It's just a different environment, so be intentional about keeping your energy level just as high as if you were standing in front of them.

Avoid a long monologue where you're giving information. In a virtual room, it's easier to get distracted and harder to stay focused. It takes a different type of energy to pay attention; a physical environment has more going on to keep people interested. Keep your presentation short and concise, and break it up with interaction, polls, videos, or short breakout sessions.

Make sure the agenda and objectives are clear right up front. Let people know exactly what will be covered, when you'll wrap up, and any expectations you have for participation. Then end the meeting exactly on time, which shows respect for their schedules (and builds trust because you keep your promises).

If you're using a slide deck, video, breakout sessions, or any other methods, ask someone before the call to handle the technology so you can focus on group dynamics. Even if you're good at using the software, it will free you to concentrate completely on the group. (Consider asking an introvert, because they're often detail-oriented and feel honored that you've chosen them to help in a way that suits them well.)

Interacting

The most important factor in getting good engagement in a virtual session is to recognize the temperaments that are present. In any group, about half of the people will be more extroverted and the other half will be more introverted. If the world were only made up of extroverts, a lot of decisions would be made and actions taken. But a lot of those decisions might not be successful because they'd lack the depth an introvert would add. If the world were only made of introverts, they would come up with amazing ideas that could change the world—but nothing would get done.

In any meeting, most leaders toss out questions and let people respond, and the extroverts jump into the discussion. They'll share their ideas openly and quickly and can easily fill the entire time of the session. The leader goes away thinking it was a great discussion because there was so much energy in the room.

Unfortunately, it was one-sided. The best thinking of the group never surfaced because the introverts need time to process on their own. They usually don't mind sharing, but not until they've formed their ideas well. How can you make sure their input is included—especially in a virtual meeting? By being intentional about helping everyone's voice be heard in the way that's best for them. Here are a few ideas:

- A few days before the meeting, ask a couple of people to be ready to share their ideas during the meeting on the topic you'll be covering in the session. People who wouldn't normally speak up usually welcome the chance to share their ideas when they've had time to prepare.
- Tell people at the beginning of the session that you'll be asking for input from volunteers later on and might even call on a few people. At the same time, make sure they know that if they do get called on, they have permission to say "Not yet." That lets everyone know they're working on their thoughts and will have something to share a bit later.

- If appropriate, tell everyone there will be an assignment due a couple of days after the session. Ask each person to summarize their thoughts and provide input about what was discussed, including any new ideas. That gives extroverts a chance to summarize their ideas and gives introverts a chance to process their ideas and have them heard.
- Encourage people to share their quick thoughts in the chat feature, especially if they're less inclined to jump in verbally. Introverts often have something to say but can't figure out how to get a word in edgewise. Every few minutes, review the written chat discussion and relate it to your topic.
- Jump on a virtual call after the meeting with individuals who didn't share verbally but gave you a sense they might have some good input. Keep it short, ask for their thoughts and reactions, and thank them. Whenever possible, mention one of their ideas in the next meeting and how you got it during a post-meeting conversation with them.

Many books on this topic have a lot of ideas on how to get good interaction but fail to discuss how to involve everyone in the group. Learn the best way to capture ideas from each person individually and capitalize on that approach.

Meeting mechanics

Little things can make or break a virtual session. Keep these in mind as you're running the call.

Don't waste anyone's time

It's tempting to start with icebreakers and other informal questions to get to know each other. The idea is OK, but choose a better setting. For example, one company I know has a monthly virtual luncheon for the sole purpose of connecting outside of work talk. They send out a gift card to each person ahead of time for home restaurant delivery, then invite everyone to drop in and chat during a ninety-minute virtual "open house." People can come and go as they please, and it's totally voluntary.

People are busy, and they often see meetings as an unavoidable delay in getting their work done. Keep the meeting tight and efficient to respect their time: prepare an agenda, stay on schedule, and end on time. Don't let anyone go off on rabbit trails that don't apply to the topic at hand. People find a sense of security in knowing exactly what to expect so they can build their day around it.

At the end of a meeting, never ask, "Does anyone have anything else?" If it sounds like the meeting is about to end, most people think, *No! Don't anyone say anything*. Don't fill the time just because you're wrapping up early; people see that unexpected ending time as a gift.

Establish simple ground rules

When you ask questions, encourage people to respond in the written chat rather than verbally. This keeps people from talking at length and gives everyone a chance to contribute. Then review the written ideas verbally and possibly include a brief discussion of next steps.

If you have a video component for participants to watch, ask them to view it before the meeting. Then, they can be prepared with their thoughts about it during the meeting. It might take a while for people to know you're serious, but make the discussion interesting and relevant enough that they'll feel a loss if they didn't watch it. (For example, one company requires people to attend the debriefing, but they can't contribute if they didn't watch the video ahead of time.)

Before each meeting, ask one person to keep track of the discussion. This won't be formal "minutes" that no one reads; it will be a one-page document that contains this simple information:

1. What were the main points covered in the meeting?
2. What action items have been assigned, and who is responsible for each one?
3. When are these action items due?

Always have a purpose

People want to know that any meeting will be worth their time. Make sure you have a valid reason and a clear purpose for each meeting. Never meet just because it's on the weekly schedule. Ask yourself, *What's the worst thing that would happen if we skipped this meeting?* or *Are there any better ways to accomplish the same thing?* If it's not essential to meet, either cancel the meeting or cut the time in half.

Be careful of recording a virtual meeting. Many participants will be more hesitant to share if they know their words will be preserved for others to see and hear. If there's a section where you want to capture people's input, tell them you'll be recording that section. Turn on the recording when that section starts, then turn it off at its end.

Do everything you can to stay conversational. By their very nature, virtual meetings tend to bring an added layer of formality that doesn't happen in person.

If you want to help people be more productive and less distracted in a virtual environment, consider hosting a collaborative virtual meeting at a certain time each day for a couple of hours. People can jump into that room where there won't be any discussion about anything—just a chance to work with other people doing the same thing. It's kind of like going to a library to study. You don't have a lot of distractions, and everyone tends to stay focused in that environment. There will always be a few people who join every day, while others will drop in when they're working on a deadline.

Master the Virtual Room

It's not difficult to master the skills of reading any room, even virtual ones. Learn the basic skills (from part 2) and how to apply them. Then experiment in new environments to gain confidence.

The result? Whether you're leading the virtual meeting or are simply a participant, your simple actions can be a catalyst for changing things in that room—and people might not even realize it's happening.

That makes you an "unofficial leader" of any room!

CHAPTER 13

Leading by Influence from the Front of the Room

> Be clear, be brief, be quiet.
>
> Riaz Meghji

Someone said that there are two kinds of people in the world:

1. Those who are comfortable speaking in front of others.
2. Those who aren't.

That's quite a generalization because a lot of us fit into both categories, depending on the situation. Some people feel at home on a stage before an audience but struggle to respond when they're called on in a small team meeting. Other people excel when they're presenting information to their boss in a one-on-one conversation but would be terrified if asked to present it to the entire department.

The first group is by far the smallest group, made up of people who look forward to the chance to talk out loud. The second group is the largest—maybe up to 90 percent of us—who start to sweat when we're called on to present. That's why comedian Jerry Seinfeld once suggested that at a funeral, most people would rather be in the casket than giving the eulogy.[1]

No matter which group you're in, this chapter is for you. You might be comfortable when you're presenting to others, and you do it often—but that doesn't mean you're as effective as you could be. Sometimes comfort keeps us from growing our skills and making more of an impact, so we need to discover how to make more of a difference with our words.

You might be more inclined to listen than to share out loud because it feels safe. But everyone has to make presentations from time to time:

- You've been asked to present the work you've been doing to one hundred people at a conference.
- You're interviewing for a job and need to present your skillset and experience with confidence.
- You're meeting with your boss to request more funding for your project.
- You run into your company's CEO in an elevator and want to sound intelligent.
- You're called up to the front of a large meeting without warning to share your expertise about the topic.
- You've been listening for a while in a department meeting, and someone asks you, "So, what do you think?"

In these situations, your skill at reading a room quickly (and the people in it) becomes invaluable. If you're good at talking, you can make even more of an impact. If you're reticent to share, you can find your voice without fear.

When you're reading the room and acting on what you see, you're making a difference. We defined leading as "influence," and there are some simple steps you can take to make presenting and speaking in front of others your most valuable tool for effectively communicating.

This isn't a course in how to be a public speaker—there are plenty of those around. Instead, you'll learn easy-to-master skills to be effective in any situation. Confidence can become your norm. Your perspective can shift from "I *have* to speak" to "I *get* to speak." You'll no longer find speaking up to be a stress-producing experience. Instead, you'll see it as an impact-making opportunity. You'll experience the reward of using your position of influence to help others think and act differently.

In other words, you'll turn your focus outward instead of inward. When we worry about what others think of us, we focus on feeling good about ourselves and our performance. When we focus on the impact we can provide for others, we pay attention to them instead of ourselves. When that happens, we won't have time to be concerned about ourselves because we'll be focused on impact.

Too Many Eyeballs

Years ago, I was at a restaurant for lunch and had already been seated at a table quite a ways from the door. I was waiting for the person I was meeting to join me, so I kept looking for my friend to enter so I could wave him over. After about ten minutes, a man seated at another table between me and the door stormed over and said, "What's your problem? Why are you staring at me?" I hadn't even noticed him, but he thought I'd been looking at him the whole time.

That was awkward.

What would you feel if someone (or everyone) in a restaurant turned and stared at you? Most of us would begin to wonder if there was something wrong with our appearance that we didn't know about, or what the other person was thinking. At the least, it would be wildly uncomfortable. We're not used to being stared at in public.

That's how a lot of us feel when we're making a comment in any type of meeting. We look around the room (or screen) and everyone is staring at us. That doesn't happen in normal life, so it can throw us off our game.

Fortunately, by reading the room well both before and during the meeting, we can know how to respond in any situation with confidence. The process is simple. It doesn't matter if we're speaking with one person or one thousand; we can be grateful to have the chance to use our words to influence others. When we know our words can make a difference, we'll welcome people staring at us. If they're paying attention, we'll know we're providing value. If they don't, we'll know we're not connecting.

How do we get to a place where we welcome people staring at us? We focus on two factors: what we do ahead of the event to prepare, and how we navigate the event as it's happening.

What to Do before the Event

Preparation is the key to successful speaking. Whether it's planning carefully what you're going to say or learning about the needs of the participants, your impact and confidence will be a direct result of how intentionally you prepare for the event. If you just show up and hope for the best, you might survive—but your impact will be limited.

The three components of thorough preparation are *people*, *content*, and *environment*.

Know the people

Several weeks before every presentation, I set up a call with the leader to learn as much as I can about the people, their mindset, and their responsibilities. My goal every time isn't simply to present information; it's to meet the specific needs of the participants.

I've presented a seminar a few times for a group of rocket scientists (literally). They were responsible for shooting things into space and landing them on another planet successfully. I was told by their leaders that they were a high-energy, intelligent group of people, and I would love spending the day with them. I was also told to be careful of making too many off-the-cuff remarks that were facetious or humorous because they would speak up and challenge the truth of what I said. After all, their job was to be precise. They would thrive with facts and figures and concrete ideas more than general concepts to explore. That information was priceless as I entered the room.

Another time, I led a half-day productivity session for a group of attorneys at a prestigious legal firm. The person in charge of this group warned me that the group dynamics would be unusual, so my expectations also needed to be different. "They're all extremely competent in their particular area of law, and they're the best in the business. They specialize, but they really don't have any in-depth knowledge of anything else, so you won't have to worry about them challenging anything you're presenting," she told me. "At the same time, don't expect any group interaction. They're trained to never come across as not having an answer, so they'll never ask questions—even if they don't understand something." I was sure grateful to learn that ahead of time!

The same need for knowledge holds true for interacting in a team meeting or virtual call. Take a few minutes to review what you know about those people if you work with them or ask others for information if you don't know them. When you understand the nuances of who's in the room and what their relationships are, you'll be able to craft your ideas and comments to meet their specific needs. Think through (or ask) what's important to them, what the structure of the organization is, and what the roles and responsibilities of the group members are. Talk to several of those individuals ahead of time to understand the dynamics of their job, then interview the manager for their perspective if possible.

Executive coach Andrew Bryant wrote, "Pitching your idea, or presenting information without knowing what state the audience is in or what's important to them, is like driving on a freeway blindfolded."[2] You don't have to know everything, but you want to know as much as you can. When you have a clear understanding of the people around you, you'll feel a lot more confident.

Know the content

If you throw a few ideas together before a session without much thought, you'll tend to feel lost if the discussion takes a different path. What you talk about needs to fit what is important to the participants. If they find it helpful and valuable, you automatically have their engagement. If it's not relevant, they'll lose interest. What they need is far more important than what you want to present—in their minds. You might know the value of what you're saying, but if you can't connect it with their needs, it feels irrelevant to them.

This applies to seasoned speakers as well as reticent ones. It's not a matter of how gregarious you are or how strong your ability to interact is. Everyone needs clarity and conciseness. When you don't prepare well, the most common result is saying too much and talking in circles. That frustrates people because it wastes their time.

Whether you are making a formal presentation or making comments in a meeting, here are the essentials:

- Know the purpose of your content.
- Craft it succinctly and precisely. See if you can describe it in a single, powerful sentence, then have no more

than three quick, clarifying points to reinforce your objective.

- Don't overexplain yourself. Make your point and back it up, as quickly as possible. Then let people ask questions, which you can answer in the same format (make one point, then back it up). Let your additional thoughts come from answering their questions rather than initiating them yourself.
- Keep reinforcing your main point. Afterward, if someone asks a participant, "What was that session about?" they should be able to state that main point because it was reinforced so well.
- Imagine that you have to pay $100 for every statement you present, but answering questions is free. Keep a tight budget on what you say.

When someone asks you a question in a meeting, be careful of the tendency to build your answer as you deliver it. Take a few seconds to think, then make one single point. If you say anything else, it should only be to reinforce that point. It might leave people wanting more, so they'll ask for clarification. Again, that's a way of giving them what they want instead of force-feeding them ideas about questions they didn't have. Learn to default to answering questions instead of adding too many points. You'll get a reputation for being a clear thinker and communicator because you give those listening to you what they need.

In situations where you're giving a planned presentation, take the time to prepare it carefully. In situations where you're participating in a discussion, keep your comments concise and short, then let others ask you for more.

Know the environment

I learned a long time ago that if I visit the meeting room where I'll be presenting before a session takes place, I'm going to feel a lot more confident. When I show up for the event, I don't want to have to explore the dynamics of the room at the same time I'm getting ready to speak. If I'm able to check it out the day before and make sure everything is in order, showing up for the event is like coming home. The less I have to worry about the day of the event, the more confident I can feel about my presentation.

When I fly to another city to do a session, I always drive to the meeting location after checking into my hotel, no matter how late it is. That way I won't have to figure out my route the next morning. I can decide where to park and which entrance to use. If it's in a hotel, I tell the front desk manager that I'll be speaking there tomorrow and ask where the session will be held. Sometimes I can get into the room and look around, but even if the room is locked I can at least find its location.

If it's a meeting in someone's office, I arrive early enough to walk around the building a bit to get a sense of what it's like. I observe the layout and the "tone" of the place, thinking about what it would feel like to work there. I watch people and peek into cubicles or offices and listen to casual conversations. It doesn't take a lot of time, and I don't need a lot of information. I'm just using my assessment skills so I'm not walking into my conversation or meeting with no forethought.

The more you prepare, the more confident you'll feel. You won't be worried about your performance; you'll be looking for ways to use your influence to add to every situation you encounter.

What to Do during the Event

Whether you're speaking to a large group or just three people around a table, be intentional. Here are things to watch out for in every situation.

When you think you're losing your audience

Be interesting. It's common to think that people who disengage will look bored or irritated. Sometimes, they do the opposite so you'll *think* they're paying attention. For example, if they're sitting around tables and most of them look at you and smile, then glance down at their hands beneath the table—they're on their phones. Don't shame them; just change what you're doing to bring them back.

I once did a seminar in a room with no windows and only one light switch. Whenever I turned off the lights so we could watch a video, the room became pitch black. The first time I did so, the white tablecloths glowed like flying saucers—from the light of all the phones under the round tables. It was obvious, so I had to address it without coming down on people: "Well, I didn't realize cell phones put out that much of a glow! I'll try to step my presentation up a notch so I'm more interesting than your email."

Make sure your content stays simple and well-organized so people don't have to work to figure out what you're presenting. Observe what's happening in the room. If something doesn't seem to be connecting, slow down and simplify. Make a single point, then guide some interaction around that point.

Tell stories instead of just presenting principles—even when making a point in a small group. Author John Maxwell says, "The greatest way to express yourself is through story. I thought it was principles without stories. It was a great mistake."[3]

Keep your sense of humor. That doesn't mean telling jokes, which is always dangerous. Just keep a light approach and notice things that lighten the mood. For example, I used to teach classes at the office complex at Disneyland, which had seven conference rooms named after the Seven Dwarfs. For some reason, I was always assigned to the "Dopey" room, which provided a great opportunity for a bit of self-deprecating humor at the beginning of the class.

Build trust by checking in often while you're presenting. When you've been talking for a while, try asking, "I'm assuming these ideas are accurate—how do they match your experience? I've been telling you my perspective, but let's explore yours before we move on."

When you're nervous

Be realistic about your self-talk to make sure it's accurate.

Did you forget to tell people a key point? Your audience doesn't know what you were planning to say, so they don't know you messed up.

Did you lose your train of thought? Admit it and come back to it. If you pretend, your audience will know when you're guessing because your flow won't make sense. Always write down your purpose—the main point you're trying to make. Go back to it often to tie everything together.

Are you feeling stressed about how others perceive you? Switch your focus to helping them instead of looking good. If you help them, they'll be impressed.

Are you the leader? Greet people as they arrive the same way you would at a dinner party in your home. You're the host, so let them know you're grateful they're there.

Is the conversation getting a little rough? Look beyond the snarky comments to figure out what's going on under the surface. It's like whitewater rafting; the rapids are caused by the rocks in the riverbed, not the water itself.

Is it time to end the meeting? Don't close by asking, "Any questions?" That's an invitation for people to share nonessential trivia that doesn't relate to others. Instead, ask something like, "Based on what you've learned in your own experience and your research, how can you see yourself applying what we've talked about in your work?" You're positioning them as the expert, not you—and that builds trust.

When you're uncertain about their nonverbal cues

If someone is quiet, don't assume they're not paying attention. Someone who speaks a lot might be contributing, but they might not be listening. The quieter ones might be processing so they can shape and share their ideas later.

If someone leans back in their chair, nods a bit, smiles, and looks relaxed, they're not disengaging. They're agreeing with you.

Let other people talk first whenever possible. Otherwise, you become like a doctor who gives a prescription before making a diagnosis. Listen to people so you can understand their position, not as a gimmick to have them hear your agenda. Remember that *listen* has the same letters as *silent*.

Congratulations—You're a Leader!

Reading the room is the critical foundational skill for making a difference in any situation. With it, you gain the competence and confidence you need to know what's happening, which enables you to offer your thoughts and contribution without intimidation.

If leadership is influence, you now have the tools you need to put that influence into practice!

CHAPTER 14

Leading by Influence through Written Communication

Writing is easy. All you have to do is cross out the wrong words.

Mark Twain

There are several restaurants in various countries around the world where everyone eats in the dark. You can't see the food you're eating, the people you're sitting with, or anything going on around you. Often in such restaurants, the servers are blind or visually impaired, and the meal is designed to help sighted people experience what it's like for people who can't see. It's also a sensory experience in which one sense is blocked so the other senses are heightened for the meal.[1]

Everything we've discussed about reading a room depends on your senses. When you walk into a room full of people, it's easy to read the room. You have a great advantage because you can become immersed in the environment. You get to use all your senses to know what's going on:

- You can watch people (sight).
- You can listen to people (hearing).

- You can shake hands with people and feel physical objects like papers, chairs, and so on that are part of the room (touch).
- You can pick up any scents in the room, such as food, coffee, or construction odors (smell).
- You can snack on whatever has been provided (taste).

When you're in a virtual meeting, you're down to two senses:

- You see people on the screen (sight).
- You can listen to people speak (hearing).

If you're on the phone, it's one sense:

- You listen to them (hearing).

When you're trying to communicate through email, texts, or social media, you're down to *zero* senses:

- There's no input from the other person as you're writing, so it's completely one-sided until they respond.
- You can't see their body language or facial expressions when you're sharing, so you can't tell what they're thinking.

That's a problem because we spend a good chunk of our day processing emails. We text instead of call. We devote hours to reading and reacting to social media posts. In other words, we write a lot more than we used to and we talk a lot less. We've bought in to the idea that digital communication is just as effective for connecting as being together. But when we're writing, we've changed from having dialogue back and forth to simply typing our ideas and hitting send.

A recent study found that the average knowledge worker spends about twenty-four hours per week communicating, and almost twenty of those hours are on written communication—about half of their workweek.[2] That's why it's futile to talk about leading well if we don't consider the basics of writing well. We don't need a whole course on business writing, just an understanding of the most critical pieces of what works and what doesn't when we're putting words on a screen.

When we're face-to-face, we connect. We build relationships. We have human moments. At the same time, electronic communication isn't going anywhere. So, what are we supposed to do? What's the key to reading and leading through written communication?

Being Intentional

Digital writing seems challenging considering we don't get to use any of our senses. At the same time, it's a huge part of the way we communicate, so we can't ignore it. How can we lead people when nobody is in the room?

By being intentional.

When we're intentional about mastering a room and focusing on the needs of others, we're not showing up and hoping for the best. We enter the room with confidence, practicing the four steps—Observe the Setting, Engage with People, Plan Your Approach, and Execute Your Strategy—in every situation.

In-person settings capture our attention because we're interacting with people in real time. When we're communicating digitally, we tend to write quickly without evaluating the impact our words might have. We write our emails or posts and send them without reviewing them for mistakes—then we have to apologize for errors after the fact. How many times have we texted someone only to have our phone autocorrect to something confusing or embarrassing? It's a hint that we're not paying much attention—something that's critical for leading a room through our influence.

Being intentional means doing everything we can to ensure our written words make an impact in the absence of being face-to-face. It means that before we send any message, we put ourselves in the place of the person who will receive that message. How will they read those words? What context do they live in? What does their world look like? In other words, we *observe the setting*—the first step in reading a room.

Being intentional means treating our written conversations like spoken ones. What would the connection look like if we were sitting across a table at a coffee shop? And how can we bring that same dynamic into our written words?

Even if their writing is OK, most people rarely communicate as effectively with people digitally as they do in person. If you can be intentional about mastering the art of digital communication, you'll stand out from almost everyone else. People will read what you've written and feel like you know them, care about them, and understand them. They'll see you as a friend they can trust, not a salesperson who views them as a commission. When your email arrives in their inbox, they'll open it first.

You don't have to become a professional writer to make this happen. You simply need to learn to have real conversations with people who aren't in the room.

Let's talk about how we do that.

Leadership through Written Communication

There's a place for formal, academic writing. This isn't it.

When we connect electronically, it's similar to entering an in-person social event to connect. We want to start a relationship, not just deliver information. In the physical room, we get to talk to the people who are there. When we enter a digital room, we don't see anyone, either virtually or in person. They might not be online, so they won't see what we've written right away. When they do see it, we want them to get the same kind of feeling they would if they heard our words instead of read them: *They know me, and they care.*

You wouldn't enter a meeting, walk up to someone you haven't met, and try to sell them something. They would be offended because you treated them like an object to use, not a person to appreciate. Instead, you would approach them as a human first, then share the common ground of that humanity through simple conversation.

The same thing is true in writing. When someone reads your words, they should feel like they're having a real conversation with a real person. You're interested in what's important to them, not just what's important to you. You're usually not telling them what to do or giving instructions but rather providing encouragement so they can become better because you connected.

In other words, you're leading through your written words. You're making a difference.

Want to know if your writing is working in that way? Look at the last email you wrote and read it out loud to see how it sounds. How would you respond and feel if someone said those words to you?

Digital writing can be used for professional purposes, but it will still have the most impact when it's conversational. It's a fine line where you're trying to be relaxed but respectful. The context will determine what's appropriate. Read previous emails or articles written by that person or even from that organization to get a sense of the tone, then try to stay slightly warmer than what you read.

Ten Essentials for Digital Electronic Communication

When you're reading the digital room, write in a way that connects quickly and powerfully. You might not have the bandwidth to take a writing course, even though it could be helpful. Fortunately, there are ten things you can put into practice immediately to dramatically improve what people see and feel when they read your words (and none of them have to do with spelling, punctuation, or grammar).

1. Use fewer words

Think of how many emails and texts you get every day and how long most of them are. Make your writing concise, and it will stand out. Your readers will appreciate it, and eventually your messages will always be the first ones they open.

2. Use smaller words

You're not writing to impress people but to have a conversation with them. People use common words when they're face-to-face, so avoid using bigger words just because you're writing them. Say "use" instead of "utilize," or "many" instead of "numerous." Editor Mark Moran gives this reason: "It's not that our readers are uneducated or unintelligent. They're just really busy."[3]

3. Reread your words

In person, you can tell you misspoke by the expression on the other person's face. In writing, you can't tell. *Always* reread every message at least once before sending it. You'll catch unintentional errors and have the chance to clarify anything that's fuzzy.

4. Write to one person

Years ago, when I was in radio, a mentor told me to remember that people listen to radio by themselves, not in groups. He said, "You're talking into a microphone all by yourself, and thousands of people are listening. But they're alone, so talk to them one-on-one." This is great advice for digital writing as well. Your message might be sent to a hundred people, but each person reads your words on their own screen. Make them feel the message is just for them.

5. Get to the point

We use small talk in person to start connecting, so it's tempting to "warm them up" and "build the case" in writing before we ease into the request. Don't do that. Instead, state your point as quickly as possible so they know what you want to communicate, then flesh it out with the rest of the content. Otherwise, they might set your message aside for later when they have time to figure out what you want—or even just delete it. Your email isn't the only one in their inbox, so catch their attention by being the one who makes things easy for them.

6. Don't waste the subject line

Don't waste the subject line with generic phrases like "Quick request" or "Hope you're doing well." Start with a signal word that indicates what type of message it is, such as "Request for," or "Agenda for," or "Information about." Then summarize your message in three to five words. For example, instead of "Can you check on this?" write "Request for review of agenda." They'll know exactly what the message contains before they even start reading it.

7. Make it look easy

Since the person reading is using only their sense of sight, make your message look as simple as possible. Remember this perspective about your writing: *If it looks difficult to read, it is*. We've all seen emails or messages that are massive blocks of words. For that reason:

- Use short paragraphs broken up with plenty of white space.

- Make bullet points (like these) when you can instead of writing in paragraphs.
- In longer messages, use headings to break up the text. You want the reader to glance at your message and think, *OK, this is going to be easy to read.*

8. Stay active

Always start with the subject first, then the action. This is called *active voice*, which is the opposite of *passive voice*. People talk in active voice but often use passive voice in writing. Active voice says, "I sat in the chair." Passive voice says, "The chair was sat in by me." Put the actor first and the action second, and your writing will feel like a normal conversation.

9. Make it about them

Have you ever had a conversation where the other person talked about themselves the whole time? They thought they were communicating well because they kept the words coming, but to you it felt self-centered and unrelatable. To capture someone's attention in writing, stay focused on them—their interests, priorities, and needs. They'll feel like you care, and you've opened the door for future conversations where they'll probably ask about you as well. Whenever you present a problem, include a possible solution or two. Make sure the things you write always offer value.

10. Be nice

It's common for people to use playful sarcasm or cynical remarks in live conversations with friends who understand them well. In writing, however, such things almost always come across as negative. There's no tone of voice or body language to provide context. For any important communication, write it first and then have a trusted colleague read it for tone. "How am I coming across in this note? What mood do you think I'm in?" You can also wait twenty-four hours and reread your message before sending it. You won't be as close to it and will be able to spot the snarkiness more easily. As Alexandra Samuel advises, "Aim for online communication that makes you sound about 30% nicer than you actually are."[4]

You Can Do This

When you're writing in a digital room, you're not looking for perfection. Nobody wins the Pulitzer Prize for an email or text. You're writing to connect and communicate. You're leading the room—so you want people to think and act differently. Of all the content people have available to read, you want yours to stand out.

If you don't like the term *writing*, substitute *communicating* instead. Written words that feel tedious can be transformed into tools for building relationships and making a difference. You might even try using the talk-to-text feature of your software or device or making a recording of what you want to say before typing it. You'll have the conversational style you need and can clean up those words instead of creating them.

Remember, you're entering a room, even if it's "empty." Read it, then lead it. It won't take as long as you think to get good at this. It's a learnable skill—and even easier because you're not trying to be perfect. Keep it simple. Start small. Then grow your skills and move forward.

You're trying to lead others to become better simply through your words!

How to Serve a Room (for Impact)

The term *serve* gets a bad rap—especially in food service.

Servers have the ability to give their paying customers a great dining experience but are often unappreciated. Sometimes, those customers see them as "royal servants" and act like monarchs who expect them to provide everything they want, when they want it. They expect perfection and choose to tip poorly (or write a negative online review) if they're not satisfied.

People don't go to business school hoping to become servants. Many go in with the idea of becoming the boss and succeeding wildly in the marketplace. Others want to have strategic influence on a company by using the skills they've learned. Not many dream of a career where they just do what they're told in order to keep somebody else happy.

That's the common view of what it means to serve. A better view could energize your entire career—even your whole life.

In 2015, the concept of service took on new meaning because of an animated movie: *Minions.*

In this comedy, minions are small, yellow, pill-shaped creatures whose sole purpose is to serve. They're built for it and fall into depression when they're not able to serve. Unfortunately, their goal is to serve the most evil masters they can find. Writer Paul Asay describes how it works:

> We're not into the movie for three minutes before the narrator tells us directly what they're built to do: Serve the biggest, baddest, most evilly evildoer imaginable. Well, at least until they accidentally kill him. They serve Tyrannosaurus Rex until they accidentally knock him off a cliff.[1]

Once all their evil masters are gone, they become lethargic and unmotivated since there's no one to serve. So, three minions—Kevin, Stuart, and Bob—go on a journey to find a new evil master they can rally around.

We can admire the fact that minions are so passionate about serving, even if they're serving the wrong people. They were made for service.

In fact, so are we.

In part 1, we explored what reading a room was all about and why it mattered. Part 2 talked about how to read a room, which gives us the confidence to enter any room and know exactly what to do to handle the situation. Part 3 talked about using that confidence to lead the room (no matter what type) and make a difference for the people there. For our purposes, we defined leadership as *influence*, which means anyone can make that difference by simply being themselves—from the quietest introvert to the noisiest extrovert.

In this final part, we move from *influence* to *impact* as we explore the mindset, skillset, and toolset for serving others as a way of making a serious difference in the lives of the people we encounter. It adds purpose to our ability to read a room because we can add meaning to our skills. When we focus on the needs of others ahead of our own, it will change the entire environment for the benefit of everyone (including ourselves).

Here's what we'll cover:

The life-changing vision for serving the room

The challenge of change

Ten steps down into greatness

Legacy time

This is where it all comes together. Most people focus on meeting their own needs—succeeding, performing well, getting praise for their efforts, and reaping financial rewards. This approach flips our focus from "us" to "them," and we read, lead, and serve each room to make a difference for others.

We can make a greater impact than we could ever imagine, without straying from our own personality. If we alter our approach, everything else shifts for us as well.

It's a surefire approach to changing the world!

CHAPTER 15

The Life-Changing Vision for Serving a Room

> Service to others is the rent you pay for your room here on earth.
>
> Muhammad Ali

A few years ago, I walked into a bookstore with my granddaughter, Averie. She wanted to see if any of my books were on the shelves, so we approached a young woman at the service counter and asked.

"Could you direct us to the self-help section?" I asked. That's usually where my books are shelved.

The woman hesitated, then grinned and said, "Well, that would defeat the purpose, wouldn't it?" Clever response, and it made the point.

It's interesting that the self-help section of bookstores is usually pretty large. It probably means that a lot of us are more interested in "helping ourselves" than asking anyone for help. We're independent. We're in a culture that says, "I can do this—I don't need anybody else." If we have to ask for help, we feel like there's something wrong with us. We don't submit a job résumé that lists "needy" as one of our strengths; we want to prove that we have what it takes.

That's a problem. As humans, we're created for connection. We need each other, no matter how independent we feel. "We're all torn between the desire for privacy and the fear of loneliness," says writer Andy Rooney.[1] We want to take care of ourselves, but we need the input of others in our lives. It's usually only when we don't have that input that we realize what we're missing.

Both are important. It's the law of supply and demand. Everyone has needs, and everyone has unique abilities. Society succeeds when both of those are in play. When we have a need we can't fill on our own, we tap into the abilities of others to meet that need. When we have the abilities that others need, we're available to help them.

Stephen R. Covey suggests that most people overvalue *independence* and undervalue *interdependence*. We want to feel good about ourselves, which usually ties in to our ability to take care of ourselves without needing others. That's independence. It's not a bad thing, and it's essential if we're going to be able to meet the needs of others. It's a critical skill that makes us feel safe when we're around others.

But that's not the highest level of maturity, Covey says. *Interdependence* is when we use our *independence* to meet each other's deepest needs. Once we've developed a healthy sense of independence, it's important to start using that confidence to make a difference. If we don't, we can get stuck in our own little world, focusing only on ourselves and what makes us happy. When that happens, we rob others of the huge value we can bring into their lives—and we can't make a dent in the world.[2]

Think about a baby. Infants depend on adults to meet their basic needs. In a healthy situation, parents spend about eighteen years trying to give their children everything they need to become independent, functioning adults. We invest in them, giving them the tools they'll need for life. If they develop healthy friendships as they grow, they start to learn the value of community. If those relationships are missing, it will be tough for them to take the next steps in living healthy, independent lives. They'll constantly be reading every room they encounter to survive, not to experience healthy, mutual relationships.

Eventually, children grow toward adulthood, graduating from high school and moving out on their own. They use whatever skills they've picked up to navigate life. We use the expression "leave the nest" to describe this transition. They've learned enough to get started on their own. Over the next few years, they fine-tune their skills of living.

As they move forward, they come to a crossroads. They have the option of living just for themselves or using that independence to invest in others. Hopefully, they discover a simple truth: a healthy, fulfilling life of impact comes from investing in others.

As Simon Sinek says, "If we were good at everything, we would have no need for each other."[3] Well, we're not good at everything, so we need each other. All of us.

The Power of Connection

When I'm writing a book, I spend more time by myself than is healthy. Putting words together on a page comes from thinking, not from talking. My conversations are what produce the ideas and raw ingredients that go into the mix, and my writing suffers when that's missing. But when it comes time to choose the words and shape them into sentences and paragraphs, it has to happen alone. It's an independent activity, not an interdependent one.

When I'm working on a deadline, I also spend more time by myself than usual in order to get the project done. I feel like I can't afford the luxury of connecting with people because it will interrupt my progress. Unfortunately, spending too much time alone means there's no one to challenge my thoughts and ideas or to keep me motivated. I start believing everything I think, and my thoughts can be negative. It's easy for me to get stuck and feel unmotivated, which leads to feeling guilty and stagnant.

I need time alone to do the work. I need time with others to stay fresh and energized.

For me, that connection comes in two forms right now. One, I'm interviewing people for their stories and expertise that provide material for this book. These folks are in positions where they have to read a specific type of room, and I want to explore how they do it and what the results and benefits are.

Second, I'm meeting with people I care about to enjoy life together. There's no agenda, just connection. It's amazing what ninety minutes over coffee can do to energize me for my writing time, even though we're probably not talking about writing. I feel better and I think better.

Both conversations accomplish the same purpose: face-to-face interaction with others. Connection becomes the fuel for everything I do—and it's all based on service.

This is just as true for introverts as it is for extroverts. I'm an introvert, which means I need plenty of alone time to recharge my batteries so I can do what needs to be done. At the same time, I don't want to use introversion as an excuse to avoid connection. It doesn't have to be a noisy group of people at a restaurant; it can simply be an "introvert friendly" situation like a quiet connection with one or two safe friends (a scenario that fits the profile of most introverts).

Life is designed to be done together, not entirely alone. It's a matter of finding the right balance that gives you the most energy. It's about taking care of yourself so you can serve others.

Service requires self-care. Flight attendants always instruct us to put on our own oxygen masks before helping others with theirs. If we don't follow that order, we won't be able to take care of either ourselves or others.

The Value of Looking Outward

I grew up in Arizona, back in the days when we didn't try to protect ourselves from the sun; we tried to get more of it. That's where we get the phrase "healthy tan." If you got more sun, it was considered healthy.

As a result, these days I have a standing appointment with a dermatologist and have enabled him to drive a Mercedes. I trust him because he's extremely competent in his skill, and he wants to make my life better by getting rid of things that could threaten it.

Between appointments, I often see new spots on my skin that look suspicious. They might itch or hurt or change color or shape, so I get concerned. If I look up my symptoms on the internet, I'll start thinking about getting my affairs in order. But nine times out of ten, my dermatologist will look at each one and say, "No, that one's not a problem. But I need to do a biopsy on *this* one." And it's always a spot I never even saw. His years of training enable him to know what is a problem and what isn't simply by looking.

I asked him once, "You can look at a spot and immediately know if it's something serious, right?" He said that was usually true, though he still had to test it. But he could generally spot a big issue right away.

"So, if you're waiting to be seated at a restaurant, and you see someone near you that you're certain has a life-threatening spot that needs treatment, what do you do?" I asked him. "Do you say something? That seems a bit presumptuous and rude, but their life is at stake."

His response: "It's none of my business because I'm not their doctor. But if I can tell it's an active melanoma, I might pull them aside, introduce myself, and apologize for intruding. Then I simply suggest that if they haven't had it checked, they should probably see their doctor as soon as possible."

That's it. Minimal intrusion—but using his unique ability to impact someone's unique situation. It's not about him; it's about caring enough to serve the other person and make a difference.

Why Serve?

Serving others sounds like a good idea. But is it worth the effort? What's the payoff?

We live in a world that encourages us to focus on ourselves and our personal success. Just look at all the books and articles that tell us we need to make ourselves the priority, since that's what everyone else is doing. If we want happiness and fulfillment, it comes from going after opportunities to succeed.

True, there is a sense of fulfillment when we succeed and complete great accomplishments. But in the long run, that fulfillment is short-lived. The message is, "Look at what I've done for me." Later in life, we'll be staring at our awards and trophies by ourselves, without anyone to share our joy.

Profound joy comes when we serve others. Beyond our personal achievements, a life of fulfillment and purpose comes when we invest in the people around us. That's why serving others instead of just ourselves is a mindset change. When we make that shift, joy multiplies—for us and for the people we serve.

Service is the culmination of our skill-building journey. We need to gain the confidence that comes from growing our skills and mastering the art of making connections. When we enter a room, we want to become confident enough that we can look beyond ourselves.

With that as a base, we want to make a difference. That's where *competence* comes in. Knowing what to do allows us to focus on others, using our unique abilities to meet people's needs. Blending confidence and competence is the healthy way to build genuine connections with others.

If the idea of service feels new to you, check out the payoff:

1. *You'll get fulfillment through connecting with others.* Serving others lets you experience genuine relationships, which include a sense of shared purpose and community. When you do meaningful things with others, you get to share in the satisfaction and fulfillment that come with it. It's like a daughter who wants her parents to play with her so she doesn't have to play alone—it feels better to both parties.
2. *You'll start a chain reaction of kindness.* A ripple effect starts with a single act of service. When you serve and get the benefits, others feel it and want to serve as well. That starts a movement that tends to grow exponentially and can transform whole communities. It's an easy way to start changing the world with acts of compassion and empathy.
3. *You'll grow personally in unexpected ways.* Personal development happens naturally when you leave your comfort zone to serve others. When you engage with people who are different from you and have unique challenges, you understand the world better. It helps grow your resilience and empathy and makes your perspective on life bigger. In the process, you discover more about your strengths, what you're capable of, and the things you're passionate about. You learn to "think outside the box."
4. *You'll clarify your purpose.* You don't discover your purpose by thinking about it. You find it when you're

doing something that's bigger than yourself—serving others by mentoring, volunteering, or being with people when they need you in their lives. It's discovery by doing.

5. *You'll create your legacy.* It is easy for people to get stuck in their current situation without looking toward the future. Your everyday choices shape your legacy. Serving others with your time and talent creates the ingredients to make a long-term impact on the world. It doesn't come from your achievements as much as from the positive impact you have on the people around you. Buildings don't just appear on a street; they're created one step at a time. Our tiniest choices matter.

So yes, service is about focusing on others. But when you do, it's like a "buy one get one free" offer where the other person benefits—but so do you. That's a bargain worth pursuing!

CHAPTER 16

The Challenge of Change

> To handle yourself, use your head. To handle others, use your heart.
>
> Eleanor Roosevelt

Everybody reads the rooms they enter; they just might not realize they're doing so. It's subconscious, and they're just trying to fit in with what's going on the best they can. They have no intention of changing or influencing what's happening. They don't believe that's even an option.

There are a lot of things in life that we take for granted, assuming they won't change. When they do change, it shakes up our world because we are counting on them to stay the same. It's uncomfortable, and we scramble to figure out how to handle it.

Living in Southern California, I've gotten used to earthquakes, but I don't like them. Nobody does. We count on the earth not moving, so it's unsettling when it does. It doesn't matter what we're doing or how important it is; when the ground starts to shake, we stop what we're doing to see what's going to happen. A little shaker gets our attention. A bigger one might last ten seconds but feel like ten minutes. We long for things to become normal again so we can go on with our lives.

Whenever we walk into a room, we assume things will be similar to the last time we went there. If it's a social event, we look around to see who is attending, where the food table is, and how we'll navigate what we see. If it's a weekly team meeting, people enter the same way each week, sit in about the same places, and go through the same routines. In a family gathering, there's usually not much that changes. The happy people are probably still happy, and the grumpy people are probably still grumpy (or even grumpier).

So, why would you even want to consider making a change in the room you're in? *To make it better in some way.*

That's been the message of this book. Learning how to read a room effectively is a powerful skill to develop because it gives you confidence. You don't always have to feel uncomfortable and wonder how you're coming across to others. With basic skills and practice, anyone can become confident in any room they enter (using the four steps we learned in part 1). You never have to pretend to be anything other than you are, because that's the only way you can be effective. "Being yourself" becomes your superpower.

That skillset gives each of us the ability to impact that room in some way, big or small. By capitalizing on our newfound confidence blended with our unique strengths and temperament, we can make others' lives better because of our influence. It might be one person at a time or a number of people—it doesn't matter.

If we simply observe a room, we'll feel confident. If we stop there and don't serve that room, we've squandered an opportunity.

Think of the potential we have. Let's say we attend a meeting or social event with the mindset of engaging and serving someone, discovering what their current dreams or challenges are, and giving them a few words of honest encouragement. When they leave, they'll feel more empowered to handle their situation than when they entered the room.

Our intentional words made them stronger and better.

Because of that, they take the first few steps toward their dream. They have just enough courage to take an action step toward solving the challenge they're facing. We've provided the momentum to help them get in motion and overcome inertia. Over time, they keep moving forward and rise to a new level they had previously only dreamed of.

Does it always happen that way? Not necessarily, and we often don't get to find out the results of the impact we've had. But it happens more than we realize. People are hungry for encouragement and often feel stuck or hopeless. A few simple words can change a life, and the ripple effect means they'll be able to do the same thing for others.

Impact one person in that way, and you've changed that one person. Do it as a lifestyle, and you might change hundreds or thousands—who could go on to change the world.

Why We Hesitate at Work

"OK, I get it," you say. "It sounds good, and I can see the value of helping others. But what about me? What if nobody is meeting my needs, and I spend all my time meeting theirs? It feels like I'm going to be on the short end of this deal."

It's understandable that focusing on serving others sounds like a risk to your personal success, especially when it's been your experience for a long time. If people haven't invested in you, why should you invest in them? Where's the guarantee that they'll reciprocate?

There isn't one. But we're not looking for guarantees here; success in the world of servant leadership isn't a zero-sum game. We're banking on the evidence that shows that when we're committed to investing in others, it will come back to us in some way, at some time. Like any investment, we can't get the return until we put our money down.

To make it happen, we take the risk of going first.

Motivational speaker Zig Ziglar often said, "You can have everything in life you want, if you will just help other people get what they want."[1] Adopting a servant leadership approach to people becomes your pathway to even greater personal success.

Think of how it works in a business setting. By focusing on the needs of others, you develop a supportive and motivated team of people who work together to achieve the goals of the department. If you're the leader, your success becomes enmeshed with the team's success. When they succeed, you succeed. Working together, you accomplish more than just the sum of your individual efforts. Everyone benefits, including you.[2]

Serving others builds stronger relationships that are based on trust, which impacts your chance for personal success. When you invest in others and believe in them, they'll be more inclined to reciprocate. That produces a loyal team environment where people become committed to each other's success.

When your pattern is serving others, people notice. Your reputation grows, which opens the door for new opportunities for your own growth and promotion. That's a win-win situation, where everyone benefits. You "went first," so you were the catalyst that set the process in motion.

The One Thing You Need to Be a Servant Leader

If you want to be a servant leader, there's one thing you need: *someone to follow you.*

You might have a solid philosophy of servant leadership. But if nobody is following you, you're not a leader—yet. You're on the path, but you need to take the next step to proactively invest in others.

How do you get someone to follow you? Master your skills in reading a room, then use those skills to start making connections. You won't have to say, "Hey, would you like to be my follower?" Make a connection, care about that person, listen and explore to get to know them, then find ways to encourage them. Don't do it to gain a tribe of followers; just make it the default setting in your everyday practice, in every situation. It might seem like nothing is happening, but you're influencing people one at a time.

Followers don't generally sign up to be on your team, though some relationships grow into that. You're investing in people consistently, and it makes a difference in their lives. It's refreshing for people to encounter someone who genuinely cares, is honest and vulnerable, and doesn't have hidden motives. As Oprah Winfrey reportedly said, "Lots of people will ride with you in the limo, but what you want is someone who will take the bus with you when the limo breaks down."[3]

Be that person for others, and you'll get the support you need as well.

How to Measure Your Leadership

Too often, people focus on their own leadership abilities. They're concerned only about how well they're doing as a leader. To move into servant leadership, that focus should shift toward developing leadership in others. Show how anyone can lead in their own circle of influence. Your leadership works if others feel empowered to lead others and serve them in the same way.

One way to measure the effectiveness of your leadership in business is to see how many leaders you have created. When done correctly, people won't look at you and say, "They're the leader, I'm not." They'll say, "I'm a leader in this area, and here's the difference my influence is making." That approach gets rid of the hierarchy of leadership where you're at the top and everyone is under you. You're growing servant leaders instead of hiring them.

It works just as well outside of the office. In any situation, your goal is to have a mindset of helping people become slightly better than they were before your conversation. It's your casual but intentional words that influence them the most:

- When you're with your children, be an encouraging parent.
- When you're with friends, lift them up.
- When you're at work, consider how to give your boss the courage they need right now, in addition to your colleagues and direct reports.
- When you pick up your morning coffee, say a few kind words to the barista to brighten their day.

It's that simple. Reading the room gives you confidence. Leading the room lets you help others through influence. Serving the room helps everyone feel more human.

Anyone Can Change Any Room

If I'm not the formal leader or host of a meeting or event, the agenda and details might be out of my control. If the meeting isn't starting on time or is running over, it can be frustrating if I'm a participant. But I can't make the leaders get things moving just for me. If there's an overcooked meal, I won't go into the kitchen to complain (unless I'm in charge of the event).

Because I've spent my career reading rooms, I know there are things I can influence that the people in charge might not recognize. If the temperature is too hot or too cold or the lighting makes it hard to see a platform well or to take notes, I talk to the right people to get it taken care of. In most events, I'm looking for anything that's a problem, and I move to solve the issue.

As a participant, there are a lot of things I can't do anything about. Here's a representative list of things I *can't* control:

- The personalities of the people in the room
- The priorities of the person in charge
- What someone else is feeling or saying
- What others think and do
- The background of other people in the room and the filters through which they interpret life
- How others are feeling or getting along
- Decisions other people make

Here is a complete list of the things I *can* control:

- Me

I can't choose everything that happens, but I can always choose how I respond to those things. I can choose my attitude. If I let those things overwhelm me and ruin my day, I've become a victim. If I choose to accept and adapt to the things I can't change, I'm back in control.

I can read the room and I can influence certain things in the room—but not everything. When I choose to serve the room, I draw a line between the things I can control and the things I can't control. Then I do everything I can to make a difference where I can. For all the things I can do nothing about, I choose to let them go. My personal happiness and sanity come when I put my energy into what I can influence, not what I can't.

That's what it takes to be a leader—a person who influences their environment. They're intentional about making a difference wherever they can and not focusing on the things they can't control.

In the process, they're leading others through influence and serving others so they can do the same.

That's the value of servant leadership—in any setting.

CHAPTER 17

Ten Steps Down into Greatness

> Leaders don't create more followers. They create more leaders.
>
> Tom Peters

The staircase to greatness goes down, not up.

That thinking is counterintuitive for most of us, especially in a work setting. From the moment we get our first job as a teenager, we're figuring out how to move up the ladder of success. We get new skills and try things out and build relationships, always striving to find better opportunities to add value. We're trying to make a living while being recognized for the contribution we make. We might be promoted into management, where we're responsible for the performance of other people. We try to get them to do what we need them to do because it will reflect poorly on us if those people don't succeed.

Years later, we pick up a book like this that says that true success—let's call it "greatness"—comes from doing the opposite. Instead of serving our own needs first, we prioritize meeting the needs of others. The book says that when we do it, our own needs will be met in the process.

After all those years of moving up, it's quite a transition to think about moving down.

In the last couple of chapters, we've discovered why we would want to make that change. Whether it's in our job environment, with our family and friends, in groups we're part of, or at a social event, serving others is the key to success in relationships. Put ourselves first and we'll see others as minions to help us reach our goals. Put others first and we'll change the way we relate to everyone.

I have studied a number of books and articles about what it takes to genuinely serve others. There were so many things required that most of us would close the books and dive into a bag of chips. After some reflection, I realized I could combine those suggestions with my own experience over the last few decades and distill ten character traits I'll call "the non-negotiables." None of them are difficult, and none relate to certain personalities more than others. Most are just a matter of changing our mindset and thinking in a new direction, then practicing that mindset in our relationships.

Want to become world-class at serving others? Here's where to put your focus (in no particular order).

1. Deep Listening

In almost any setting, people aren't used to someone listening deeply to them. Deep listening means to practice being undistracted during every conversation. People should feel like they're the only one in the room, and you make that happen by being intentional during each conversation. Ask questions, then let them respond without rushing. Follow up with another clarifying question (or two) about what they said, which you can only do if you've been paying attention.

If it's hard for you to remember details of conversations, consider capturing the key ideas in writing. Before you see them again, review those notes briefly so they're fresh in your mind. It shows care and respect when you're able to bring up something you discussed a few days later, either by asking another question or just asking how it's going.

Get in the habit of carrying a small notebook with you or jotting things down on your phone. Anytime someone says something that captures your interest, say, "Wait—that's really good. Let me write that down." It affirms the value the other person brings to the conversation to have someone capture something they've said. If you can, bring up their insights in a team meeting when it's an appropriate fit.

2. Genuine Humility

Country singer Mac Davis sang, "Oh, Lord—it's hard to be humble when you're perfect in every way."[1] Those words hint at the danger of humility; if you think you have it, you probably don't. If you start getting it, you can easily become proud of it, and then it disappears.

Humility means considering the needs of other people above your own. That doesn't mean your needs aren't important; you just prioritize them differently. They're called "needs" because you need them. But you're not using other people as the main way to get your own needs met. If you concentrate on helping others get what they need, they'll often do the same in return.

When everyone is out to take care of "number one" (me), relationships are based on taking. We're all trying to get others to take care of us. When humility comes into the picture, relationships become all about giving. If everyone focused on giving, everyone would get their needs met in an atmosphere of mutual care and respect.

Is that realistic? Not totally, since you can't force people to feel in a certain way. But if you, as the leader, demonstrate this humility in your own life, it can become contagious.

3. Consistent Curiosity

Most people accept the way things are without questioning them, whether personally or professionally. If you want to serve others, you'll need a different approach: being curious. No matter what it is, if you think you're familiar with something, dig deeper. Get in the habit of asking the question every four-year-old asks about everything: "Why?"

Get curious about the people you want to serve. Learn about their priorities, interests, and needs, connecting with them enough to know them below the surface. Your goal isn't to tell them what to do but to help them excel in every relevant area. Study their personalities and communication styles so you'll be able to connect in their language. You don't have to pry into every detail of their life or become best friends, but work to discover the big picture of who they are as a person. You'll be able to anticipate their needs and tap into their unique genius.

When you demonstrate curiosity, it builds your brand as someone who cares. It can't be artificial, because people will sense it. Whether it's something a person says, something you read, or something that's been announced, get in the habit of asking "Why?" and "What else?" and "So what?" It takes practice initially, but it will enable you to become a caring leader as you find out what matters most to those around you.

4. Authentic Gratitude

In a glass-half-empty world, we're used to people taking things for granted. If they win the lottery, they complain about the taxes due. If they're given a promotion at the office, they only think about how much more work they'll have. When they receive a gift, they're disappointed in the color or size.

I held a door open for someone last week, and they didn't acknowledge it. I know it wasn't required, but it felt odd and a bit rude to have them ignore my gesture. Maybe it feels routine when someone says "Thank you," but we notice it when it doesn't happen.

A few days later, I held the door for someone else. As they walked through, they looked me directly in the eye and said, "Well, thank you. That was very kind." It didn't make me feel proud of myself, but I felt a shot of encouragement that we had a simple, genuine human moment.

Having a filter of gratitude changes the way we approach the world around us. Sure, there's plenty to complain about—and it's real. Gratitude doesn't overlook the negative; it just balances it out with the positive. It helps us see things the way they really are, which always includes a mix of good and bad.

It also impacts our ability to serve others. Those small human moments build up and connect us to each other in positive ways, developing trust and appreciation. It's hard to feel completely negative about someone who expresses genuine gratefulness in challenging situations.

5. Intentional Growth Mindset

It's easy to assume that the way people are is the way they'll always be. After all, if they wanted to change, they would have done it before now. It's not just others we feel that way about—it's ourselves.

If we want to serve others, we need to start with our own mindset. Our results are the byproduct of our choices. If we want new results, we can make new choices. When we recognize the reality of that in ourselves and the people we want to serve, we have a new filter that shows us the potential in everyone—even if they don't see it themselves. Each conversation we have can be an encouraging nudge to help someone believe in themselves and make new choices in new directions.

Seeing through a mindset of potential is foundational for helping people grow. When they can't believe in themselves, they can borrow our belief in them until they get their own. We become cheerleaders in the highest sense and build an atmosphere where everyone has the vision of becoming better today than they were yesterday.

President John F. Kennedy said, "A rising tide lifts all boats."[2] The context was that if the economy got better, everyone would benefit. In the same way, creating a mindset of growth in any group of people impacts everyone in a positive way.

6. Abundant Empathy

Forbes senior contributor Dr. Tracy Brower writes, "Empathy is the most important leadership skill according to research."[3] Another *Forbes* contributor, Alain Hunkins, gives the details: "Employees with highly empathic senior leaders report higher levels of creativity (61%) and engagement (76%) than those with less empathic senior leaders (13% and 32% respectively)."[4]

This one's simple: *empathy* (through service) means caring about others in ways they can feel and accept. It makes people feel seen and heard in conversations, which results in a variety of benefits:

- Empathy helps you understand people's needs, concerns, and perspectives, connecting with them in a way that builds trust.
- When people trust their leader and know they have their best interests in mind, they become more positive and collaborative as they work together.

- By understanding people, you can customize the way you support and guide them toward personal and professional growth.
- Communication with empathy has less conflict and fewer misunderstandings.
- People work together better when everyone feels valued.
- Motivation is a natural byproduct of empathy.

Empathy can't be faked. If you don't have it naturally, it's worth the effort to learn how to bring it into your relational toolbox.

7. Clear Vision

When you think of a servant, you think of someone carrying out the wishes of another person. That looks different when you're practicing servant leadership with your people. You're not doing whatever they want. You cast the vision, either your own or that of those above you. Your people need empowerment to carry out that vision.

It's not their job to figure out where everyone is headed; that's your job. You keep the vision clearly in mind, then motivate the team to get everyone there. The traditional approach is to know where you need to end up, then tell people what to do in order to get there. In servant leadership, you find ways to inspire them with the vision so they're motivated to find the best way to achieve the goal. A famous quote says, "If you want to build a ship, don't drum up the men to gather wood, divide the work, and give orders. Instead, teach them to yearn for the vast and endless sea."[5]

Whether it's at work or in a personal setting, avoid telling people what they need to do to better their lives; they'll resent it. Simply inspire them with the possibilities they might not have considered.

8. Competent Character

It will be difficult to serve other people, especially those you have some responsibility for, if they don't trust you. In other words, *character* is critical to servant leadership.

At the same time, people need to believe that you know what you're doing if they're going to follow you and trust your ability to get them where they need to go. In other words, *competence* is also critical to servant leadership.

Service means you want the best for your people. You can't make that happen if you're missing either character or competence. If you are highly skilled at what you do but don't have personal integrity, people will think you're competent but won't be convinced you have their best interests in mind. If you have the highest character but your skills aren't the best, people will like you but won't trust your ability to take them where they need to go.

We've defined leadership as *influence* for the purpose of this book. When you have both character and competence, your influence will grow because you've earned trust. When trust is high, you can serve people and motivate them to grow—and they'll welcome that type of service.

9. Chronic Consistency

We run our lives on things we can count on:

- A chair we use every day has never broken, so we sit on it without worry.
- Our car starts every morning, so it throws us off when it doesn't.
- The train shows up every day on schedule, so we count on it—until it's late.

We build trust in people, things, and circumstances when they're consistent. If an employee shows up on time every day (or calls in if something happens), we're concerned when they're an hour late. We're not angry, just worried. It's not what we've come to expect.

When you're trying to serve others, they know if they can count on you to be consistent. If you are, they'll relax and trust you. If you're not, they'll never develop that trust because they don't know what to expect.

How do you build consistency? It's fairly easy, but it takes intention:

- Keep your promises. Do what you say you'll do.
- If there's a legitimate reason why you can't fulfill an expectation, that should be the exception rather than the norm. Consistent leaders always find ways to come through on their commitments. When a problem arises, let people know early and honestly. If you're stuck behind an accident on the freeway and will be late, call immediately and let someone know. If you wait until you arrive late to explain yourself, you've been inconsistent and damaged trust.
- When you don't act with consistency, apologize sincerely with no excuses. Just say, "It was my fault—I could have left earlier."

10. Crafted Collaboration

If you want to influence the people around you and be focused on their needs and priorities, it takes more than building trusting relationships with each person. It means becoming a catalyst of those trusting relationships between everyone in the group. You'll be modeling it through your individual relationships, but it might not come naturally to others. Find creative ways to help people learn to respect and value each other so the workplace becomes a safe environment for everyone. You want people to arrive at work each day excited because they're working with people they trust to accomplish things that matter.

That doesn't mean everyone in the room will become best friends. That can't be legislated. It means people will learn how to collaborate with those who think differently than they do and might have different ideas of how something should be done. You can be the person who moderates those dynamics, publicly and consistently celebrates the contributions each person makes, and handles issues quickly as they come up. If you don't, the group will assume you're playing favorites because you handle different people differently.

To serve in a way that motivates others to do the same—that's a great goal for a leader.

Your Simple Plan for Success

These ten character traits are nonnegotiable, but you don't have to have them all in place to be successful. Consider using these as your personal growth plan as you learn to serve others. Take them one at a time, perhaps spending a week focusing on each one. Read that character trait's description each morning that week, then make it a filter for your day. You might even set an alarm on your watch or phone every ninety minutes so you can quickly check in. *How have I done in this area in the past ninety minutes? What worked that I could continue doing? What didn't work that I can do differently going forward?*

After ten weeks, repeat the process. Each round will bring you closer to the type of leader you want to be—one who influences others from a life of personal integrity. In other words, you're becoming what you want others to catch and start implementing in their own lives.

Remember, you can't fake this. People will sense it and won't completely trust you. It's not a set of steps to carry out; it's a change of thinking that permeates everything.

You'll be serving people for all the right reasons, and other people will change because of your influence. You'll be making the difference you were designed to make!

CHAPTER 18

Legacy Time

What do we live for, if not to make life less difficult for each other?

George Eliot

I've always struggled with the idea of self-help books.

That's a problem because that's the section of the bookstore where all of my books are found. Those books have been successful because people have life challenges they need help with. They could go to a therapist to work through issues or a life coach to find new strategies. They could talk to friends to see what they would suggest. But often their first thought is, *I wonder if there's a book out there that might help.*

So, they go online or head to a local bookstore to see what's available. They look for recommendations and reviews, then narrow their search down to something that looks like a good fit. Fortunately, one of my books has often been the one they grab when they need help with relationships or communication. They see one of my titles like *People Can't Drive You Crazy If*

You Don't Give Them the Keys or *How to Communicate with Confidence* and think, *That's what I need.*

These readers are trying to "help themselves" before reaching out to others, like a homeowner with a leaky faucet grabbing a wrench. It seems quicker and easier than other options, so they feel like it's a good place to start. I've read hundreds of self-help books for that very reason, and they usually give me some great nuggets of wisdom to consider and try to implement.

It's good—but it's a poor substitute for having other people involved. It's like a toddler who wants to be self-sufficient, saying "I can do it all by myself." Maybe they can, but it's not a great strategy for living a fulfilling life.

If I spend my whole life helping myself, I get to the end of my life alone. I've invested in me, but nobody is paying much attention. I haven't made a difference in anyone else's life.

Making that difference is what we call a *legacy*. It's the fingerprints we've left on other people when we're gone. It's the people who are different because they were involved with us.

Start Sloppy, but Start

Author and speaker Jon Acuff says, "Be brave enough to be bad at something new."[1] Common sense tells us that the first time we do anything, we won't be amazing at it. Somehow, we have this desire to be perfect right up front, so we set an impossible standard. When we're bad at something, we can get discouraged and give up.

If you haven't yet learned how to read a room effectively, you are not alone. We all know how it feels. For some, it's a lack of confidence. For others, it's a lack of impact. In either case, you won't read these first few chapters and suddenly take control of every room you enter. It'll feel sloppy at first, and there's the tendency to think, *I'll never get this down.*

That's OK. In fact, expect to feel that way. Just realize that though the beginning feels sloppy, every new attempt to practice your skills makes you a tiny bit better. Sloppy starts are exactly where the most impactful people in the world began—but they kept growing.

That's what happened with United Airlines captain Alfred C. Haynes. In 1989, the tail engine of the DC-10 airplane he was flying exploded, severing all of the plane's hydraulic systems that controlled flight. In other words, all of the controls became useless and there was no way to fly the plane. The only thing he could do was increase and decrease the speed of the right and left engines in an attempt to keep the plane from spiraling. There was no way to direct anything else in the flight. It was an impossible situation.

Long story short: Captain Haynes managed to approach a runway in Sioux City, Iowa, where the plane crash-landed and burned. But at age fifty-seven with thirty thousand hours of flight experience, he managed to land the crippled plane in a way that saved 184 people out of the 296 aboard. It was still a tragic loss, but his years of experience enabled him to avoid a total disaster.

Official reviews of the accident showed that the primary reason for the survival rate was Captain Haynes's long experience in the air. He had honed his skills to the point that he didn't just fly the plane; he sensed everything that was happening based on his intuition and instinctively responded. He wasn't using just his knowledge of flying but also his finely tuned reactions that were automatic, based on his many years in the cockpit.[2]

Captain Haynes was undoubtedly a sloppy pilot on his very first time in a small plane with a flight instructor. Everyone is a sloppy pilot on their first flight. But he learned and practiced one thing at a time, never realizing just how far he'd grow beyond the sloppy beginnings. Eventually, his skill would save many lives.

Reading a room might not seem as important as saving lives. But the more you do it, the better you'll get at it—and the bigger difference you'll make. It's a skill you'll use the rest of your life—and will give you confidence in every situation.

Start at the End

Who will cry at your funeral? I don't remember where or when I first heard that question, but it caught my attention. At the end of my life, who will be sad that I'm gone? Better yet, who will think of me with gratefulness because I cared about them and helped them become who they are today?

It's been said that at your funeral, people won't remember all the things you've accomplished and the awards you've won. They'll remember how you made them feel.

What a great exercise! Stephen R. Covey calls this principle "Begin with the end in mind."[3] It's easy to get caught up in the busyness and demands of each day, but where is it taking you? Take time to think of the people you've been connected to and picture them attending your memorial service. How will each of them feel when they think about you?

If it's not what you're hoping for, what needs to change? What can you do differently to make an impact on others that will change them forever?

That's been the focus of this book—possibly an unexpected one. You picked it up because you wanted to learn the skills of entering different rooms and situations and feeling more comfortable. You needed the confidence a first responder has when they arrive on any scene, and you wanted to know what to do in every situation.

You've done that. The skills were surprisingly simple and just had to be customized to your unique personality. You don't have to pretend to be someone you're not; you get to be yourself, and that's what makes it work. People become comfortable with you and even like you. But as Covey says, "People spend their whole life climbing up the ladder of success. But when they get to the top, they realize the ladder is leaning against the wrong wall."[4]

You can become an expert in reading a room, but that alone won't change the world. As you've learned, you also need a sense of mission and purpose. You've explored how to take your newfound confidence and influence the people you meet, making them better than they were before. Then you expanded your mindset to one of consistent, intentional service. You learned how to be totally yourself while changing people's lives.

If you change someone's life, could we assume they might be grateful at the end of yours?

We need more than self-help books. We need "other-help" books. We need a mindset of making a dent in the world, one person at a time.

CONCLUSION

Dan Miller, author of *48 Days to the Work and Life You Love*, was a personal mentor to thousands of people through his writing, podcast, coaching, and mastermind program. Countless people have been able to escape a mediocre life and become who they were designed to be through his influence.

I only met him once, and we talked over lunch for about thirty minutes. His sincere, positive approach to life was contagious, and I felt better about "me" after spending time with him. It was a privilege to have a taste of what so many others had feasted on for years.

In 2023, he was diagnosed with pancreatic cancer and passed away after only forty-eight days. In a video he recorded about midway through that journey, he talked about his legacy. He wasn't looking for a monument with his name carved on it or a building named after him. Here's what he said:

> My legacy is in you—the people I've had the privilege of interacting with over all these years . . . sharing the principles that I learned from past masters of achievement that I know you now have within you that you can pass on and share with people that

> you have influence with. That's my legacy. . . . You now be the encourager of somebody who needs it.[1]

The good news is that it's never too late to start the journey of impacting others. If you have one conversation today that brightens another person's day, you've taken a step in that direction. Become a master of reading rooms. Then learn to lead those rooms with your mastery of influence. Over time, you'll be involved in a life of service that ripples out further than you can imagine.

Booker T. Washington said, "Those who are happiest are those who do the most for others."[2]

Anyone can do this. *You* can do this.

This is your chance; go make a difference!

ACKNOWLEDGMENTS

This morning, I went back and read through the acknowledgment pages for all nine of my previous books. I wanted to make sure I didn't repeat myself in who I thanked and what I said.

That was an exercise in futility, since the same names show up in every book. There are always a few new names, but most are people who have simply been in my life for a long, long time. They don't sit in the room with me when I'm writing; that's something I do in solitude. But they've been the ones who've believed in me or shaped me or supported me or challenged me or did all those things over the years. What I write comes out of who I am. Who I am comes out of the connections I've had with people for decades. My words exist because of those who walk with me on my journey.

Family members are always top of the list. My wife, Diane, is the most influential person in my life. She believes in me and encourages me and keeps my impostor syndrome from spiraling out of control when the pages stay blank for too long. My kids, Tim and Sara, sit with me over coffee and talk about how life is supposed to work. Their spouses are committed to the people I love the most, and I love them for it. My six grandkids ask the questions nobody is supposed to ask, which keeps me honest and challenged and grounded in reality. They're the reason I think the way I do (and provide plenty of stories to write about).

Then there are the professionals who come alongside to make sure my writing works. Rachel McRae has been my editor for a couple of years, and she holds the reins of the entire project. She knows how to steer wild horses. Vicki Crumpton has been my editorial partner since the beginning and has taught me how to put words together coherently so you don't get bored. The two of them make up my Dream Team that keeps my fingers on the keyboard.

My publisher, Revell, is where it all happens. The team has moved from professional contacts to colleagues to friends, and they're wicked smart and wildly competent. They know how to make my stuff look good and put it where you'll see it. They're the wonder-makers.

The friends who have shaped me are the ones I've known the longest. If I tried to list them, I'd forget some important ones. If you're one of them, you know who you are—and you know the influence you've had by simply doing life together with me. If you think you're on this list, you are. Just know how much you're appreciated and thanked.

I never realized the impact readers like you could have until you started contacting me with your thoughts. Consider yourself acknowledged too. Your fingerprints are on this book in ways you don't even know. All of you have impacted my thinking, and it has turned into ideas and words that now exist in this book. Your encouragement is priceless and usually comes when I'm considering an alternate career in plumbing. For all of you, I'm grateful!

Knowing that you've been affected by words I put together alone in a coffee shop motivates me to put more words together.

I'm thankful that I even have the opportunity to be on this journey together with you.

God is my life. Take Him out of the equation, and the whole thing falls apart. I write because He gave me the desire, the drive, the skill, and the opportunity. I love the whole business of writing because He plopped it onto my path and into my heart. He's the gift I'm most grateful for.

NOTES

Chapter 2 Master Your Mindset

1. Carol S. Dweck, *Mindset: The New Psychology of Success* (New York: Ballantine Books, 2016), 6–7.

2. Steven R. Covey, *The 7 Habits of Highly Effective People* (New York: Simon & Schuster, 1989), 94.

Chapter 3 Master the Process

1. BetterHelp Editorial Team, "The Advantages of Attractiveness and How It Impacts Success," BetterHelp, accessed April 17, 2024, https://www.betterhelp.com/advice/general/the-good-the-bad-the-ugly-why-attractive-people-are-successful/.

2. Saul Mcleod, "Maslow's Hierarchy of Needs," Simply Psychology, January 24, 2024, https://www.simplypsychology.org/maslow.html#What-is-Maslows-Hierarchy-of-Needs.

Chapter 4 Master Your Perceptions

1. "Heritage," Zenith Electronics, accessed April 17, 2024, https://zenith.com/heritage.

Part 2 How to Read a Room (for Confidence)

1. "Vince Lombardi: 'Practice Does Not Make Perfect. Only Perfect Practice Makes Perfect,'" The Socratic Method, accessed April 17, 2024, https://www.socratic-method.com/quote-meanings/vince-lombardi-practice-does-not-make-perfect-only-perfect-practice-makes-perfect.

Chapter 6 Observe the Setting, Part 2

1. Nick Morgan, "Debunking the Debunkers—the Mehrabian Myth Explained (Correctly)," *Public Words* (blog), July 23, 2009, https://publicwords

.com/2009/07/23/debunking-the-debunkers-the-mehrabian-myth-explained-correctly/.

2. Gerard I. Nierenberg, *How to Read a Person Like a Book* (Garden City Park, NY: Square One Publishers, 2010), 8.

3. Nierenberg, *How to Read a Person Like a Book*, 8.

4. Mark Twain, "Truth Quotes," Twain Quotes, accessed April 17, 2024, http://www.twainquotes.com/Truth.html.

5. Geoff Beattie, "Body Language Books Get It Wrong: The Truth about Reading Nonverbal Cues," The Conversation, March 28, 2023, https://theconversation.com/body-language-books-get-it-wrong-the-truth-about-reading-nonverbal-cues-201418.

6. Helene Kreysa, Luise Kessler, and Stefan R. Schweinberger, "Direct Speaker Gaze Promotes Trust in Truth-Ambiguous Statements," *PLoS One* 11, no. 9 (September 19, 2016), https://doi.org/10.1371/journal.pone.0162291.

Chapter 7 Engage with People, Part 1

1. Gillian M. Sandstrom, Erica J. Boothby, and Gus Cooney, "Talking to Strangers: A Week-Long Intervention Reduces Psychological Barriers to Social Connection," *Journal of Experimental Social Psychology* 102 (September 2022), https://doi.org/10.1016/j.jesp.2022.104356.

Chapter 8 Engage with People, Part 2

1. Oxford Learner's Dictionaries, s.v. "small talk," accessed April 17, 2024, https://www.oxfordlearnersdictionaries.com/definition/english/small-talk.

2. Adam Jaworski, "Silence and Small Talk," in *Small Talk*, edited by Justine Coupland (London: Pearson Education, 2000), 110–31.

3. Alison Wood Brooks and Leslie K. John, "The Surprising Power of Questions," *Harvard Business Review*, May–June 2018, https://hbr.org/2018/05/the-surprising-power-of-questions.

4. Dale Carnegie, *How to Win Friends and Influence People* (New York: Pocket Books, 1936), 93.

Chapter 9 Plan Your Approach

1. "Zig Ziglar Quotes," Brainy Quote, accessed April 17, 2024, https://www.brainyquote.com/quotes/zig_ziglar_617761.

2. AJ, "148 Quotes by Earl Nightingale," Elevate Society, accessed April 17, 2024, https://elevatesociety.com/quotes-by-earl-nightingale/.

Chapter 10 Execute Your Strategy

1. Taegan Goddard, "Work the Room," Political Dictionary, accessed April 11, 2024, https://politicaldictionary.com/words/work-the-room/.

Chapter 11 Leading the Room

1. Nils Parker, "The Angel in the Marble," Medium, July 9, 2013, https://nilsaparker.medium.com/the-angel-in-the-marble-f7aa43f333dc.

2. Brené Brown, "Dare to Lead Hub," Brené Brown, accessed April 17, 2024, https://brenebrown.com/hubs/dare-to-lead/.

3. The John Maxwell Company, "7 Factors That Influence Influence," *John C. Maxwell* (blog), July 8, 2013, https://www.johnmaxwell.com/blog/7-factors-that-influence-influence/.

Chapter 13 Leading by Influence from the Front of the Room

1. "Seinfeld-Public-Speaking," YouTube video, 0:27, uploaded by ExplainIt-Studios, January 26, 2014, https://www.youtube.com/watch?v=yQ6giVKp9ec.

2. Andrew Bryant, "How to Read the Room on Zoom," *Self Leadership* (blog), January 16, 2022, https://www.selfleadership.com/blog/how-to-read-the-room-on-zoom.

3. "John Maxwell on Story," *Author Coaching* (blog), accessed April 17, 2024, https://www.authorcoaching.com/blog/john-maxwell-on-story.

Chapter 14 Leading by Influence through Written Communication

1. Wikipedia, s.v. "dark dining," accessed April 16, 2024, https://en.wikipedia.org/wiki/Dark_dining.

2. Grammerly Business, "The Unofficial 4-Day Workweek: How Ineffective Communication Is Costing Your Business," *Grammerly* (blog), January 24, 2022, https://www.grammarly.com/business/learn/state-of-business-communication-research/.

3. Mark Moran, "Business Writing: Know the Big Words but Use the Small Ones," LinkedIn, March 9, 2021, https://www.linkedin.com/pulse/know-big-words-use-small-ones-mark-moran/.

4. Alexandra Samuel, "Using Social Media without Jeopardizing Your Career," *Harvard Business Review*, July 20, 2015, https://hbr.org/2015/07/using-social-media-without-jeopardizing-your-career.

Part 4 How to Serve a Room (for Impact)

1. Paul Asay, "The Servant's Heart of the Minions," *Watching God* (blog), December 9, 2015, https://www.patheos.com/blogs/watchinggod/2015/12/the-servants-heart-of-the-minions/.

Chapter 15 The Life-Changing Vision for Serving a Room

1. "Andy Rooney Quotes," Quote Fancy, accessed April 16, 2024, https://quotefancy.com/quote/1391189/Andy-Rooney-We-re-all-torn-between-the-desire-for-privacy-and-the-fear-of-lonliness-We.

2. Covey, *7 Habits of Highly Effective People*, 48–53.

3. "Simon Says: A Collection of Quotes from Simon Sinek," Simon Sinek, accessed April 16, 2024, https://simonsinek.com/quotes/.

Chapter 16 The Challenge of Change

1. Kevin Kruse, "Zig Ziglar: 10 Quotes That Can Change Your Life," *Forbes*, November 28, 2012, https://www.forbes.com/sites/kevinkruse/2012/11/28/zig-ziglar-10-quotes-that-can-change-your-life/.

2. Editor, "Why Investing in People Should Be a Top Priority for Businesses," *The Yale Ledger*, June 1, 2023, https://campuspress.yale.edu/ledger/why-investing-in-people-should-be-a-top-priority-for-businesses/.

3. As quoted in Tal Gur, ed., "Lots of People Want to Ride with You in the Limo, but What You Want Is Someone Who Will Take the Bus with You When the Limo Breaks Down," Elevate Society, accessed April 16, 2024, https://elevatesociety.com/lots-of-people-want-to/.

Chapter 17 Ten Steps Down into Greatness

1. Mac Davis, "It's Hard to Be Humble," *It's Hard to Be Humble* (Casablanca, 1980), LP.

2. John F. Kennedy, "Remarks in Heber Springs, Arkansas, at the Dedication of the Greers Ferry Dam, October 03, 1963," The American Presidency Project, accessed April 17, 2024, https://www.presidency.ucsb.edu/node/236260.

3. Tracy Brower, "Empathy Is the Most Important Leadership Skill According to Research," *Forbes*, September 19, 2021, https://www.forbes.com/sites/tracybrower/2021/09/19/empathy-is-the-most-important-leadership-skill-according-to-research/.

4. Alain Hunkins, "Why Leading with Empathy Is More Important Than Ever," *Forbes*, April 18, 2023, https://www.forbes.com/sites/alainhunkins/2023/04/18/why-leading-with-empathy-is-more-important-than-ever/.

5. As quoted in Richard Bolden, "A Yearning for the Vast and Endless Sea: From Competence to Purpose in Leadership Development," paper presented at the Air Force Leadership—Changing Culture? Conference, RAF Museum, London, July 18–19, 2007 (University of Exeter), accessed February 1, 2023, https://business-school.exeter.ac.uk/documents/discussion_papers/cls/372.pdf.

Chapter 18 Legacy Time

1. Jon Acuff, "Be Brave Enough to Be Bad at Something New," Jon Acuff, August 3, 2020, https://jonacuff.com/16081/.

2. Wikipedia, s.v. "United Airlines Flight 232," accessed April 17, 2024, https://en.wikipedia.org/wiki/United_Airlines_Flight_232.

3. Covey, *7 Habits of Highly Effective People*, 109–66.

4. Covey, *7 Habits of Highly Effective People*, 112.

Conclusion

1. "A Special Message from Dan Miller," YouTube video, 4:03, uploaded by Dan Miller, December 29, 2023, https://youtu.be/7B_2ECWgSS0.

2. Booker T. Washington, "Those Who Are Happiest Are Those Who Do the Most for Others," Pass It On, accessed April 17, 2024, https://www.passiton.com/inspirational-quotes/7630-those-who-are-happiest-are-those-who-do-the.

DR. MIKE BECHTLE (EdD, Arizona State University) is the author of ten books, including *People Can't Drive You Crazy If You Don't Give Them the Keys*, *Dealing with the Elephant in the Room*, *It's Better to Bite Your Tongue Than Eat Your Words*, and *The Introvert's Guide to Success in the Workplace*. A frequent speaker, Bechtle lives in California.

CONNECT WITH MIKE:

WWW.MIKEBECHTLE.COM

@MikeBechtle

A Note from the Publisher

Dear Reader,

Thank you for selecting a Revell book! We're so happy to be part of your life through this work.

Revell's mission is to publish books that offer hope and help for meeting life's challenges, and that bring comfort and inspiration. We know that the right words at the right time can make all the difference; it is our goal with every title to provide just the words you need.

We believe in building lasting relationships with readers, and we'd love to get to know you better. If you have any feedback, questions, or just want to chat about your experience reading this book, please email us directly at publisher@revellbooks.com. Your insights are incredibly important to us, and it would be our pleasure to hear how we can better serve you.

We look forward to hearing from you and having the chance to enhance your experience with Revell Books.

The Publishing Team at Revell Books
A Division of Baker Publishing Group
publisher@revellbooks.com